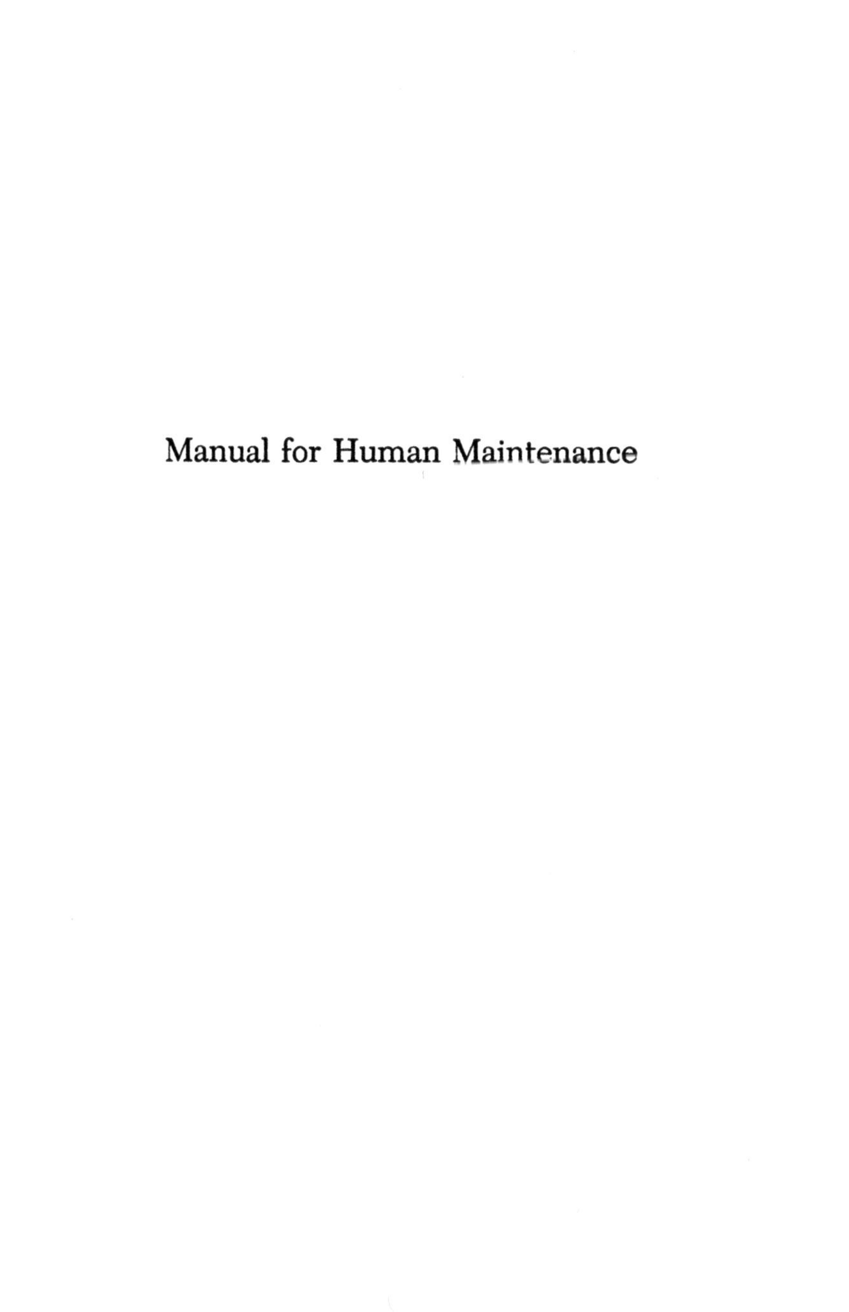

Manual for Human Maintenance

MANUAL *for* Human Maintenance

ROBERT C. MORGAN

BROADMAN PRESS
Nashville, Tennessee

Unless otherwise noted, Scripture quotations are from the Revised Standard
Version of the Bible, copyrighted 1946, 1952, © 1971, 1973. Scripture quotations marked (KJV) are from the King James Version of the Bible.

Library of Congress Cataloging-in-Publication Data

Morgan, Robert C., 1948-
  Manual for human maintenance.

   1. Christian life—1960-   . 2. Conduct of life.
I. Title.
BV4501.2.M5845 1988   248.4   87-23930
ISBN 0-8054-5053-X

For Linda, Todd, Lauren, and Rob,
whose love inspires me to work harder on myself

Preface

When I was a teenager, one of my favorite television shows was "Twilight Zone." One episode was the story of a man against whom machinery rebelled. The man's television set, automobile, air conditioner, radio, lawn mower, any and all mechanized parts of his world, stayed broken down or in need of repair. The machines had a will of their own, and they seemed to will that the poor fellow never have a moment's peace. It was a quiet, insidious revolt by lifeless gears, cogs, wires, nuts, and bolts. That story was a modest precursor of today's sophisticated science fiction stories where computers rebel or take over.

There is a sense in which that "Twilight Zone" episode was about me or, at least, I grew into the role of the poor unfortunate in the story. I am not mechanically inclined and, as a result, live in dread of machinery revolt. In particular is this true where my automobile is concerned. I overreact—tend to make too much of its ills.

Me: "What's wrong with it?"
Mechanic: "It's the universal joint."
Me: "*Universal*! Oh, no!"
Or,
Mechanic:: "Your car's jumped time."
Me: (*Panic stricken*) "Oh, my gosh! (Pause) Is that possible?"

Though nature (or my upbringing) did not prepare me for metric wrenches and the know-how to use them, it did compensate by giving me other skills, *people* skills. I am a better than average mechanic when it comes to working on (with) people. People are such an exciting challenge and so filled with surprises, I have little or no interest in dumb machines. My philosophy, deeply influenced by my all-thumbs handicap, declares that machines exist to serve people. For that reason, I do not change the oil in my car every three thousand miles or rotate the tires every five thousand. And I am certainly not going to buy one of those fancy "bags" to slip over it to keep tree sap and bird droppings off while it's parked in the yard. If I did that, would I not be serving a machine?

People, however, are a different matter. We are made to serve God. Indeed, we have certain God-like qualities about us, qualities such as freedom, creativity, knowledge of good and evil, and, especially important to this effort, imagination. We are capable of endless responses, stratagems, tricks, wiles, and monkey business. I had rather work on people anytime! But because we are so much more complicated than machinery, and because most of our parts cannot be replaced, "fixing" and maintaining us is quite a challenge. This is especially true of that part of us which makes us what we are: the spiritual variously called heart, soul, anima, psyche, pneuma, or even reason.

I hope the pages which follow encourage you, the reader, to work on yourself and to develop your Christian imagination, taking responsibility for your personal maintenance. I hope they challenge you to become a "people-mechanic" by working on the one person you know best. That, of course, is you. And if you can keep yourself hitting on all cylinders as a person, stay fine tuned as a human being with plenty of get-up-and-go, these pages will have served their purpose.

ROBERT C. MORGAN
Fish Trap

Contents

1

Three Toughies

Where your imagination is concerned, allow me to set forth three words: *recognition, motivation,* and *imagination.* They will rise before you like jagged mountain peaks. These are three of the most difficult peaks you could ever climb. If you are interested in bringing your inner resources to bear for problem solving, you will have to approach the three with the caution of a trucker with a load of nitroglycerin. The reason the three will seem so difficult is that most of us are accustomed to miracle drugs; short-term medical treatment; and turning ourselves over lock, stock, and barrel to physicians for cure. Thus, we sometimes lack the discipline and know-how to solve our own problems. Certainly I have "ills" with which only I can deal. Doctors are able to treat the body, but the spirit remains immune to penicillin. Nagging personal problems have to be dealt with in solitary confinement for the most part. All our personal resources are needed.

Recognition

Generally speaking, Joe and Josephine Average are very adept at pointing out somebody else's faults and shortcomings. They are not nearly as capable where their own persons are concerned. Jesus gave us the all-time great image of that truth in the Sermon on the Mount: the fellow with the two-by-four poking out of his eye trying to remove a cinder from the eye of his neighbor. For the Averages, self-awareness has always been in shorter supply than the blind spots in their personalities and behaviors.

One has to be self-aware to recognize oneself as a gossip, as prejudiced, or as greedy. The reason more of us are not is because we have defense systems which deny reality. These surround our ego and the truth about us like a fortress. Our defense systems are always working, and they help reduce anxiety. They are, in that regard, essential to survival. These same defenses are not helpful, however, if they keep us from making needed adjustments in our behavior.

For example, if I want to be athletic and coordinated but am fumblesome and awkward instead, I can still pretend I am a football or baseball hero. I might even daydream about my heroics on the playing field. This is a type of *denial,* and it helps relieve my anxiety about my real self. To that point, it is not hurtful. If, on the other hand, I begin bragging about my abilities in sports and making up lies about those abilities, my denial becomes a problem. Job did some of this wishful thinking when in chapter 29 he reminisced about his happy past, when his state and estate was blessed, as opposed to the reality of his then-present suffering.

Suppression is a conscious effort to prevent an impulse or thought from being expressed. In Luke 2:19 we're told the virgin Mary, upon hearing the report of the shepherds about the multitude of angels, "kept all these things, pondering them in her heart." This is a type of suppression. Repression, however, is a strong unconscious defense mechanism. It is a barricade against allowing the unmentionable to achieve consciousness. It's hard to find a suitable biblical example of repression. If we speculate—pure speculation, mind you—we could say Saul of Tarsus might have had leanings toward Christianity before his Damascus-road experience. Sympathies with "the Way" may have been so shocking to the young Jewish bulldog that he repressed them. He may have forced those thoughts and impulses into exile from his conscious mind. Because Saul couldn't acknowledge these sympathies, he might have had dreams about following Christ, dreams filled with symbols: fish and water and doves and stark, dead trees which miraculously budded. Then, on the Damascus road, this neglected material suddenly broke into awareness in a dramatic way. That's speculation to explain the way repression works.

Displacement is a defense we use when we react against a secondary or substitute object. This takes place when a man kicks the family dog rather than

his wife against whom the anger is actually directed. It is easier and safer for a pastor to scream at
his children than the chairman of deacons. A busi-
nessman is more likely to mouth off to his wife than
his boss. A wife may take out her frustrations by
beating a rug rather than her mother-in-law. In
Genesis 4, the story of Cain and Abel, Cain's anger
and frustration may have been directed at himself,
his bad luck or Yahweh. But the older brother dis-
placed his negative emotions, heaping them onto
the younger, and eventually killing him. Cain
probably thought it was safer to commit mayhem
against Abel than Yahweh!

When we seek to justify unacceptable behavior
or thoughts, we resort to *rationalization.* In Genesis 3:12-13, when the Lord God asked if the man
had eaten of the forbidden tree, the man respond-
ed, "The woman gave me the fruit!" When God
turned to the woman, she said, "The tricky serpent
made me do it!" Thus was born the most handy
rationalization ever for religious folk: "The ol'
devil made me do it!"

Projection, on the other hand, takes place when
we attribute a personality trait which actually be-
longs to us to someone else. Take, for example, the
parable of the Pharisee and tax collector praying in
the Temple (Luke 18:9-14). The Pharisee, a religious peacock, looked at the lowly tax collector and
gave thanks that he was not like that fellow. In
truth, however, every vile thing the peacock read
in the other fellow had a foothold in himself. By
projecting his own religious bankruptcy and vile-

ness onto the lowly tax collector, the Pharisee was able to strut and exult in his personal religiosity.

Regression is a return to an old behavioral pattern. Take Simon Peter as an example. If he were as hot blooded and impetuous as has often been surmised, after years as a disciple of Jesus, he momentarily regressed to old ways when he cut off the ear of one of those attempting to arrest Jesus (John 18:10).

These defenses and others make seeing ourselves as we are difficult. They falsify the data. They click on automatically the moment we feel anxious, threatened or insecure. For that reason, an individual cannot easily gain perspective where personality and behavior are concerned and the way these are perceived by others. Furthermore, these defenses mean the gospel emphases regarding confession, repentance, and conversion involve earthshaking dynamics that reach far beyond walking down the aisle of a church. I have difficulty seeing the need for confessing my sins when I am telling myself, "I'm no worse than the next guy!" (rationalization). The need for repentance is difficult to acknowledge when I act highhandedly and refuse to acknowledge my dark side (denial, or maybe even repression!). Conversion seems unnecessary when I live a life in which the spiritual dimension of my being is unfed (suppressed). Not many people want to hear the words of the prophet: "We have all become like one who is unclean, and all our righteous deeds are like a polluted garment" (Isa. 64:6). Such a recognition involves a form of death, which is exactly the way Jesus described Christian discipleship (Matt. 10:39).

Motivation

Quite frankly, the word *motivation* scares me! I know people can be motivated to change their behaviors and do so with just a word. After all, radio and television advertisements do this all the time. But motivation, it seems to me, remains the weak link in problem solving and bettering our life situations and reaching our potential. People come to me for counseling who know they have problems and disorders and need to make changes. My experience, however, has been that few are highly motivated to do what is necessary to change their situations. Sure, they feel good having a nonjudgmental and sympathetic ear listening to their stories. And sometimes, after several sessions of counseling, a person will find the proper motivation. (That's a goal of counseling!) But more times than not, at the time of counseling, these folk are not sufficiently motivated to do what needs to be done.

Even Jesus had a problem with motivating people. Jesus' nonviolent ways and personal example did not stop Simon Peter from regressing to his old cut-and-slash routine. When the brothers Zebedee, with their mom acting as spokeswoman, asked Jesus for places of honor in the kingdom, the Master instructed them about the relationship between servanthood and greatness (Matt. 20:20 *ff.*).

Yet, in the opening chapters of the Book of Acts, these same brothers, as representatives of Christian Judaism, remain in Jerusalem with the other apostles awaiting the restoration of the kingdom to Israel (and no doubt hoping for administrative posts in the new government!). What about the Pharisees or the rich young ruler? Or the multitudes of Jerusalem over whom Jesus lamented (Matt. 23:37)? He was unable to motivate them to change old ways and habits for new ones.

Thus, a question creeps up on me as I write these lines. How many people out there are sufficiently motivated to overcome that crisis or correct that personality disorder or behavior problem? The woods are full of folk who want the benefits without the bother, the gain without the pain. And, if I could offer a money-back guarantee of success, that would motivate some to go to work on themselves.

Motivation is an *inner* desire to mediate the conflicting tendencies within one's person. It is a want-to proposition: "I want to do something about the incompatible parts within me." For that reason, the language of motivational psychology is chocked full of words like *stimulus, response, habits, drives,* and *desires.* In the final analysis, however, it all comes down to changing a negative, counterproductive activity for a more positive and productive one. Consequently, if you have scaled the peak of recognition, peeled away your defense mechanisms like a banana skin, at least enough to claim a measure of self-honesty, then you must decide whether you are adventurous enough to take on "Motivation Mountain."

Imagination

So, you are honest with yourself. And you are motivated to change your self-defeating ways. But can you make it over the peak of imagination? That is what you will be asked to do in the following pages. Discipline and training are required to develop one's imaginative capacities, to see and experience what is needed.

Imagination is the mind reaching out to create mental pictures of situations and conditions not actually experienced firsthand. The late R. G. Lee called it "picturizing." When he preached, he pictured in his mind the events from Jesus' life, death, and resurrection. This is a capacity everyone possesses to one degree or another (except the brain injured). Artists and writers usually have the most fertile imaginations, mainly because they exercise this capacity. Imagination is a Godlike endowment that can lead us to better and enrich ourselves and the world in which we live.

Consider the following pages as you might the script of a play. The playwright writes the words, but the scenery, movement, and little pieces of "business" which make the drama work are the task of the director. In the pages ahead, you are the sole actor and director and should take note of the following guidelines.

First, the exercises ahead are not intended as one-time efforts. (Get that "hypo" mentality out of the way now!) It takes repeated effort to form mental pictures. You can rotate the tires on or change the oil in your automobile faster than you can make graphic mental images. After all, an automobile is a dumb machine. You are a person and infinitely more complex!

Second, you will need to withdraw to a quiet, comfortable place to exercise your imagination. You cannot initially work on you with your mind cluttered and your body geared to the next earthly pursuit. Later, with discipline and practice, you might be able to, but not in the beginning. Also, you will find it helpful to keep your eyes closed as you exercise and strengthen your imagination.

Finally, imagination (and the attending quiet and discipline and focusing of energies) can enhance prayer and meditation. When you turn aside to work on you, do so with the thought that yours is a godly pursuit. And remember that in Jesus the Son, God the Father, performed the most imaginative feat ever: He became a person like you. That means being a person can't be all bad! That is reason enough to practice preventive maintenance on yourself.

2

What to Do When You Lose Sight

Forgetfulness

In the rooms of my soul-house are people who move about freely. These spiritual tenants are there not by permission but by something more irresistible. They have rights, the rights of heritage and ancestry; because they have supplied the materials necessary to make the dwelling which is me, they demand to be seen and heard from time to time. They are permanent residents; so they open windows, plunder in the basement, and make soft footfalls on the dark staircase at will. Their presence is not an imposition, and most of the time, their footfalls are indistinguishable from my own. As a matter of fact, I have to work at being aware that my soul-house is not a hermitage, but a great hall, tall and wide gabled.

One of these tenants is my great, great-grandfather, a Baptist pastor who preached for nearly fifty years in southwest Alabama. He was born in a log cabin in 1836. Reverend, as he was called, fought in the Civil War. Somewhere around

1894, the eldest of Reverend's nine children took a bride, my great-grandmother. Grandma and her farmer husband (who died in 1898 of typhoid fever) had two children, a son and a daughter. The daughter was my grandmother, my father's mother. Just before Christmas in 1919, Grandma's only daughter married a dapper young man. My father was born a week before Christmas 1924.

I know many interesting stories about these family members. Reverend accidently burned down the family cabin and all its contents when he was six years old. Grandma remarried and had another son, Joe, who died in 1960. My father's father served in World War I and underwent surgery that left him with the palsy. My father was a career military man who retired to his hometown, where people seemed to reserve a special affection for him.

My mother's mother was a will-o'-the-wisp whose weight hovered around ninety pounds. She worked as a nurse for many years. Even when I was fourteen, she could outwrestle me, though I once broke her rib when I surprised her from behind. Mother's father was a woods foreman at the sawmill, and he sang in the church choir and liked square dancing. Pop and I watched "Gunsmoke" together.

I was born on May Day, 1948. A week before Christmas in 1949 my sister, Anna, was born. Nearly ten years later, Kathy was born. Tolstoy observed that all happy families look alike while each unhappy family is unhappy in its own way. The five of us, parents and children, always felt we had been chipped from that indistinguishable mass of fortunate families.

My mother was stable and reliable and possessed a great faith. Hers was and is a quiet beauty which draws people and sometimes makes them depend too much on her, a curse for one who has trouble saying no. There was none better at cherishing than she. She worked and cultivated the small world of the family as effectively as my father did the larger world outside.

After all those years of beating the odds as a warrior—World War II, Korea, Vietnam—my father fell to a cancer diagnosed in late 1972 and, in March of the fallowing year, was laid to rest in the ground disturbed only by the whistle of bobwhites. Johnny joined Reverend, Grandma, Papa, and other pilgrims of the town. Home to stay.

These are just some of the spiritual tenants who inhabit my soul-house. These are by no means all. There are many people and factors whose imprint I will presumably bear forever. Such it is for each of us. To know where one is going, one must know where one has been. This involves something about which the Old Testament makes much: *remembering.*

Through the Passover the Jew annually remembered the most important historical event in the nation Israel's experience: the Exodus from Egypt. The Passover feast was a reliving of the nation's birth and rise from slave to chosen son. Later, in

Babylonian captivity, the psalmist looked back and remembered:

> If I forget you, O Jerusalem,
>   let my right hand wither!
> Let my tongue cleave to the roof of
>   my mouth,
>   if I do not remember you,
>   if I do not set Jerusalem
>   above my highest joy! (Ps. 137:5-6).

The Jew remembered lineage and genealogy and tribe. Family was the cornerstone of society, and one of the Commandments placed honor for father and mother as an obligation on one and all. To neglect one's heritage was to be directionless.

> Remember the days of old,
>   consider the years of many
>   generations;
> ask your father, and he will show
>   you;
>   your elders, and they will tell
>   you (Deut. 32:7).

This is a book about "mechanicing" on oneself. It is about working on character disorders and self-defeating ways. It is about taking charge of oneself. Yet, therein lies the paradox. The human shuttlecock is in endless flight between the hard overhand of determinism and the deft dropshot of free will.

I respect Calvinism, but I insist on human free will. Aldous Huxley stated the former in stark terms. He said some people are born victims, born to have their throats cut just as surely as the cut-throats are born to hang, all of which are visible in their faces. What that means, I think, is that sometimes, in spite of the incredibly bad taste of it all, we throw people to the lions. We feel that genes or environment or both are stacked against them, and they, in turn, are foreordained to act out some tragic script or dance a fool's jig.

That is why I respect Calvinism. It is hard to escape genes and environment and breeding, as the patterns which repeat over the generations prove. We are most familiar with the idea of history repeating itself in the families of alcoholics or in abusive families. The truth is, however, none of us ever gets very far from those who birthed us. Like it or not, we carry a lot of people around with us; they, like a dried creek bed, guide our trickle of water along a course carved by the generations.

Religion can, and often does, provide the key to breaking out of this determinism. To my way of thinking, religion is the best vehicle for change and, therefore, self-direction and free will. I am not overly optimistic about change apart from religious experience. What most of us call change amounts to little more than a clean handkerchief in the breast pocket of a soiled and crumpled suit. The overall effect is still frumpish. Genuine change is a new suit with socks and shoes to match. That kind of change involves the breaking of the contours and shapes of the generations, the ability to mediate the disputations of the voices in the soul-house. Real, genuine, productive change, life-altering change involves the development and strengthening of a personal voice, what might be called an increase in "self-mass." Thus, change and the exercise of free will are Herculean undertakings whose starting point Augustine prayerfully described this way: "O Thou, from whom to be turned is to fall, to whom to be turned is to rise."

Even the most self-directed of us came from some place. We are born into a certain environment. Certain individuals influenced us with their values and judgments and opinions. For one reason or another, we sometimes divorce ourselves from our past. We forget where we have been. Sometimes the past is painful. To not be aware of it, however, is a mistake. To forget—to fail to *remember*—is to be incomplete.

The most miserable people I encounter as a minister and counselor are those who have forgotten or neglected their heritage or past. They have neglected values learned and seem unaware of the people who still roam around in their soul-house. They have blocked out important parts of themselves with greed, self-pity, anger, prejudice, or shame. Pieces of themselves are missing, left behind in their hometowns, churches, schools, and with families and friends.

Thus, before you attempt to work on yourself, be certain that all your "parts" are there. Your problem or disorder may be the result of neglect of the past, where you have been and the things with which you have been indelibly imprinted. (I'm talking inerasable and unfading!) Perhaps your forgetfulness is making you unhappy.

Some years ago, I participated in a seminar with marriage and family counselors and hospital chaplains. One of the group was leading us in an experiential exercise in which each was to relax, close his eyes, and put himself in that one place where he knew beyond a doubt he had met or experienced God in some way. As I relaxed and closed my eyes, I wondered where I would place myself. After only a few effortless seconds, I saw the green water, the pines, the boats, the deep blue sky, and the lone fisherman on the bank.

The place was the pond located a mile or so from my hometown. I fished there as a boy and teenager. As a teen, I often went there to be alone and try to sort things out. I was trying to cope with a heightened sense of existential anxiety during those years. In the isolation and quiet, I often found momentary solutions which, when strung together over the years, reached like a fragile bamboo bridge over the canyon of purposelessness I felt within. There, at the pond, I heard the voice of God many times.

Sometimes I dropped my tackle and went into the stand of pines in the southwest corner of the dam and knelt on the canopy of brown needles and pleaded to be delivered from my fears. At other times, downcast and dragging, I would go to the pond in a light rain and sit on the bank under a willow tree and let the rain wash away the blues. Whether the cork bobbed was inconsequential. Things became visible in the rain. Once I saw a doe swim the pond and, seconds later, the dog that was chasing her. There were birds with stilt-like legs, birds created so as not to mind wet feet. There was the 'gator, armor-clad and gliding no where in particular, a Monitor looking for a Merrimac.

There is something essentially spiritual about fishing anyway. Dark, goose-pimply water, bobbing cork, solitude, the reprimand of a redwing blackbird, the swirl of a bass, the slow watery track of a snake crossing in the heat of noon, the expectation of a nibble, the hope of the catch—one more cast, one more good lookin' spot—all these imprint the brain. There the impressions are transformed into the spiritual stuff that make human beings different from what swims or flies or crawls. There, like a more perfect language, the impressions become the great eternal themes of life and death, aloneness versus the unity of all things, fear, promise, perseverance, luck, and lucklessness. A fisherman can acknowledge the God of creation for His marvelous and diverse ways, give thanks for the azure depths and oranges of the bluegill, and the depthless green of the largemouth, then cuss or praise Dame Fortune for her stinginess or generosity on a particular day.

Back to you. Perhaps you are forgetting a part of yourself, and it is making you unhappy. And since you will repeatedly be asked to use your imagination, do so now as you go in search of your "holy space."

Begin by getting comfortable and quiet. You can sit or lie down, but it might be best to get in a position where you can recline your head. Do not cross your legs or ankles. Do not cross your hands upon your chest. Do not put weight on any part of your body. Relax and make your mind a blank slate, as clean as possible. (It's hard! All kinds of things will try to crowd in, but give it a try.) When you are ready, try to envision that one place in your past where you experienced God. This can be anyplace at all, anyplace, but it must be a place where you once felt the presence and love of God breaking through. It might be your childhood church, the one you left years ago. It might be your parents' dinner table or your grandparents' house on Christmas Day. It might be when you were alone, walking in the woods or sitting in a favorite chair in a room no longer there.

Wherever or whenever this "holy space" was, notice as many details as possible. Who was there, if anybody, other than you? What was the occasion? Were there any particular smells or tastes or sounds you recall? Did anything important precede or follow the moment? How did you feel right then?

Take it all in! There are a thousand details you might recall.

Go ahead! Take the psychic/spiritual train home. It might be the first time you have done so in ages. Goad your soul to remember who you are, where you came from, and how you learned that God is.

3

A Broken Heart

Sorrow

The variations on a broken heart are as numerous as the stars in the Milky Way, as countless as the grains of sand on the seashore, as limitless as humankind's potential for hurt and pain.

The world is filled with star-crossed lovers. Take the time to try to imagine them as a great hurting multitude, row upon row of people needing people. You'll probably need to close your eyes to gain a mental picture of them. Do your best to imagine. You may not be able to envision such a throng. You may have to concentrate on something smaller, like the feeding of the five thousand. Maybe you can see no more than a hundred representative souls, or even one archtype representing millions. But imagine what you can and pay attention to as many details as possible: dress, facial expressions, posture, manifestations of hurt. What does it feel like to be in the presence of that much pain? You might even watch for familiar faces in the crowd.

Here is a single woman in love with a married

man. She knows that Timing—that poker-faced middleman—has taken away her chance for happiness by a cruel prank. He has not permitted her to find the man of her heart until it was too late. The loved one is forever out of her reach.

Over there is a young man whose overtures go unheeded by the young woman he loves. She just does not feel the same way he does.

Back there are two people who do love each other, but there are things which keep them apart: their careers, ideals, values, social standing, maybe even their politics.

See that man? He is divorced. He still loves the woman to whom he was married for fifteen years, but it just did not work out. And both of them tried.

And what about that seventy-eight-year-old woman who just lost her husband of fifty years?

See that person? He is thinking about what might have been; thinking about a certain person he knew ten, twenty, forty years ago and how different and fulfilled life might have been with her.

In actuality, the multitude extends as far as the eye can see and beyond. It is the fellowship of pain and aching hearts. But brokenheartedness extends beyond lovers. The variations, again, are endless.

A mother stands at the bedside of a dying child.

A man is fired from the job into which he poured his productive years.

A young woman learns of her infertility.

A son is excluded from his father's will.

A candidate for foreign mission service is

notified that she has been turned down due to medical reasons.

A pastor is forced to resign his church.

An eighteen-year-old's dream of being maid of honor at her best friend's wedding is not going to be.

A wife learns of her husband's infidelity.

A nine-year-old has to repeat the third grade.

Broken hearts are made from the stuff of important and inconsequential things. The criteria is hurt, disappointment, and the feeling that justice has somehow not been served. If you have a broken heart, you will never be alone. There will always be company aplenty. As a matter of fact, most of those who belong to the fellowship will go unrecognized. You may sidle up to one on your favorite church pew, or be fitted for shoes by one, or even work alongside one. This is all the more reason to treat even a stranger with civility and compassion.

But given the fact that you are a part of that sad-eyed, granite-faced, aching number, and that your number is legion, what are you going to do with *your* grievously injured heart? (Please note that by asking you to imagine the great assemblage of the brokenhearted, and to think of yourself as one of the many, I have circumvented certain statements most likely to be repeated in the throes of self-pity, namely, "Nobody's ever experienced this before!" and "Nobody's ever hurt like this before!" If you need to assure yourself of your uniqueness, however, please feel free to use these.

You can catch up later!) To begin with, time has a way of taking care of a sizable portion (maybe most!) of broken hearts. Just by holding on and letting time pass, a heart can mend. Remember puppy love and high school crushes? The heartbreak of that lost job may, in time, prove to be a boon. Only time will tell.

But then, some sorrows hang on and hurt, making us feel they are here to stay. If yours is one of these (and they all seem that way initially!), what are you going to do about it? Allow me to suggest a plan of action.

Sit down in a chair in a favorite place and make yourself as comfortable as possible. Close your eyes and relax, taking as much time as needed. With your mind cleared and your body tension free, cup your hands in your lap and imagine your own hurting, broken heart in them. That's right! Do it! If possible, you'd permit a physician to hold it and apply some kind of medical epoxy to its brokenness. And the doctor wouldn't understand your heart half as well as you! It is about the size of a fist and fits nicely into your cupped hands. If you try hard enough, you can feel it beating—throbbing. Or, you can hold it with one hand and place the other over it in a protective way. With the heart completely surrounded, you have unhindered access to its beat and hurt.

When you can feel your heart in your hands— when you can feel the hurt—let it serve as a reminder of your own aliveness. Let the pain validate that you are. Pain is proof of life. And where there is life there are endless possibilities, a million eddies sweeping us this way and that, into this cove and out again. If you were dead or if you allow your broken-heartedness to dull your prospects for living, your possibilities for service to God, humanity, and the world would be nil in the first instance, minimal in the second.

With the awareness that you are alive and, based on the presupposition that life is preferable to death, that pain can be helpful, meditate upon the brokenheartedness of God. The Gospel writers said that the sorrow of the Father was manifested in darkness the day Jesus, the Son, died. That black day, however, gave way to the crowning event of the Christian faith: Easter Sunday. Now it is time for you, with the Father's help, to plan for your own "resurrection." (Actually, yours will be more a coming alive but the principle is basically the same.)

Maybe your heartbreak or sorrow is so great that you will need some time in the tomb, some time to grieve. That's OK. Some hurts are deserving of such. As soon as you are able, however, it is imperative that you plan for your return, maybe even mark the day on the calendar. Nothing is more fundamental to Christian faith than the belief that the empty tomb prevails over the place of the skull. So, too, must it be for you. Remember: If you choose to remain in the tomb of brokenhearted-ness indefinitely, all that will be taken up are your bones and what might have been. But it is Godlike to make plans in the darkness, to push at the weight of immovable stones, to make something out of emptiness.

4

When Your Nose Is Out Of Joint

Aggravation

The language of aggravation is among the most colorful in the English language: "rub salt in the wound," "pour oil on the fire," "add fuel to the flames," "tread on my toes," "go against the grain," "rub the wrong way," "get under your skin," "get his goat," "set her teeth on edge," "stick in my craw," "grate on his nerves," "drive nuts or bananas," "drive up the wall," "get your back up."

Perhaps the reason we have so many colorful expressions is because there are so many aggravating people in the world. Ever notice how many of them you know? Or how they tend to congregate in your church? And what about that one person who drives you up the wall and rubs you the wrong way and sticks in your craw? You know, that person who has no other calling in life except that of putting your nose out of joint!

As a people-mechanic, I marvel that Jesus, the Master people-mechanic, managed to deal with so many people without letting them get under His skin. The Bible does not tell us about all the whiners, manipulators, gossips, passive-aggressors, and paranoids He must have encountered. One would think there was sufficient aggravation in the disciple band alone, what with the upwardly mobile James and John, the conniving Judas, and the impetuous Simon Peter. Yet He dealt with them all and multitudes more and only rarely got His back up. When He did, it was not aggravation like ours, paltry and out of control. He did not brood and seethe and plot mayhem. He got aggravated at misguided religion, willfully blind eyes, and the thwarting of God's intentions. With Jesus, aggravation apparently never got down to attacking individual personalities.

I do not mean to imply that people are the only aggravations in life. Balancing the checkbook and Form 1040 can result in hair pulling, too, as can a thousand and one other nonpeople factors. Yet, aggravation from family members, friends, and acquaintances tends to be most intense and long lasting. So let us concentrate on human relations.

To begin with, take some time to conjure up a mental picture. I said *time*. It takes that to develop your Christian imagination. If you are a "Type A" personality—always on the go, goal oriented, and plagued with a sense of time running out on your every enterprise, your Christian imagination may have no more depth than the stony ground in the parable of the soils recorded in Mark 4:1-8. If you doubt there are Christians with little or no imagination, take a look around, that is, if you can find the time! Besides your Christian imagination suffering from your inability to be still and concentrate, so do prayer and meditation. "Type A" folk rarely notice burning bushes. They're too busy herding sheep, that is, as long as their health permits!

Imagine that person who aggravates you, your personal thorn-in-the-flesh. Take the time to isolate just what it is about this person which puts your nose out of joint. Maybe he is a braggadocio, a busybody, a crybaby, a faultfinder. Maybe he is too highfalutin or prone to leg-pulling. Maybe he is too much like you (it's possible, you know!) and gives free rein to a personality trait you try to repress. Maybe he reminds you of somebody out of your past: a self-righteous mother; a weak father; the school teacher who never liked you; the inflexible preacher who frightened you as a child with his sermons from the Book of Revelation. Whatever it is you find annoying in this person, isolate it.

When you know exactly what irritates you so, when you can pinpoint it rather than generalize, imagine yourself as you are at this moment. Imagine surrendering a little piece of yourself—a finger, ear, nose, eye, a pound of flesh here and there— each time the person in question annoys you. After all, that is precisely what is taking place each time your nose is put out of joint. You are granting permission to Paul or Paula Peeve to raise your blood pressure, grind your teeth, churn your stomach, and make your head pound. Moreover, you are surrendering self-determination by permitting him or her to determine how you feel, act, and respond. That ought to be your choice, no one else's. If yours has been a long-term annoyance with this person, imagine how much (or little) of you is left. Is there any of you left?

Try another exercise.

Do you remember Carlo Collodi's famous children's story about Pinocchio, the wooden puppet? Pinocchio had nose trouble too. In his case, each time he told a lie his nose got longer. Using your imagination, how long would your nose be if it grew a fraction of an inch everytime you got annoyed with your particular irritating person? Try to visualize its length. Let's add a "twist." Imagine what your nose would look like if it not only got longer with each annoyance but also crooked (you know, "out of joint"!). What would it look like? Try to compare it to something. For example, since I'm a big pasta eater, I see mine looking like the world's longest lasagna noodle, broad and wavy! Also, try to imagine the problems a nose like that would present.

If, after daily exercising of the imagination in this way, you insist on putting your nose out of joint (yes, it's your choice!), make yourself a Pinocchio nose. Everytime you get aggravated with the person in question, vow to buy some modeling clay that very day. With it, you can mold a long nose and stick it to your face. In all probability, however, it would fall off. So buy the clay and give it to a neighborhood child or the Children's Department in your church's Sunday School. After all, somebody may as well benefit from your aggravation! Or buy the clay and put it (and each succeeding can) on a shelf as a reminder that your aggravation is costing something. But buy a can each day your nose is out of joint.

Actually, there is no great secret to Jesus' dealings with people. What He did was simple but profound beyond words. He did not see harlots, tax collectors, Pharisees, or cripples. He could look beyond the trappings and folderol and see the person hiding inside.

Where Pinocchio was concerned, things turned out well. The fairy turned him into a real live boy after he had learned to be honest. Likewise, you will be more humane when you cease letting you-know-who pull your strings. Set out to find the real person hiding inside your aggravating friend or family member, and make it *your* choice to do so.

5

When Your Knees Are Knocking

Fear

Jelly legs. Thumping heart. Shortness of breath. Difficulty in swallowing. Sweaty armpits. Feeling of collapse. Anyone who has risen to make a speech knows these symptoms. These are the cronies of fear. Ever notice how fear affects us from head to toe? It makes us have "second thoughts" (the head is presumably affected). It gives us "cold feet" and makes us "shake in our boots." It makes us "chickenhearted" and "fainthearted," as well as "lilylivered." When fear arrives, we apparently quiver like a mountain of gelatin; we are "jumpy," "jittery," "edgy," "shaky," and "tremulous." All in all, fear is quite a puzzlement. It calls us to defense by keying certain physiological processes (adrenalin, for one) which give the body more energy to face a threat. On the other hand, fear makes it hard for us to think and solve problems.

Sometimes fear comes in king-size proportions. It becomes intense and attaches itself to an object or idea. When it does, we call it a *phobia*. There are all kinds of phobias: fears of confined space, high places, cats, thunderstorms, even blushing! Fears of such intensity usually require some type of counseling or therapy to overcome. But most fears are manageable without consulting a professional. Usually a person will stumble through the speech, sit down, and breathe a sigh of relief.

One of the things I notice about fear in people is that the symptoms are feared as much as the stimulus. For example, a young lady is going to sing a solo in church on Sunday morning. That is the stimulus. But listen to what she says about it.

"I just know my knees are going to be knocking."

"I'll probably have a lump in my throat and won't be able to get the notes out!"

"My voice is going to quiver or break. I just know it!"

"What am I going to do if I forget the words?"

"I'm going to be pale as a ghost standing up there in front of all those people."

None of these are pleasing prospects. This young lady is fearful of fear (and if it gets intense enough it becomes phobophobia!). She is dreading the *sensation* of fear, and that dread intensifies the experience of singing and jeopardizes her performance. It is quite a dilemma! It is also quite common.

Maybe you have one fear in your life, a fear that does not handicap you or interfere with your functioning as a person, which makes life unpleasant for you. Maybe you fear flying but manage to jet inspite of it; or escalators, but manage to escalate.

Maybe you fear a person, perhaps your boss or teacher or the gossipmonger down the street. Again, your fear is not a phobia, nor is it a free-floating anxiety that attaches itself to any and all things and makes life in general fearful. But you have one thing that stirs you up and makes you want to run away. You know, that thing you consider hurtful.

If you can isolate your greatest fear—that heart-thumping, knee-knocking stimulus—I can tell you something interesting about it. *It's only electricity, man!*

We are talking voltage here! It is a little fire dancing on your nerve endings. You can read about the technical side of the human nervous system in an encyclopedia. If you do, note the terminology. It'll probably say something about *conduction, positively and negatively charged* cells, *circuits,* and so on. It gives a whole new meaning to the term *electrifying personality!* Use your imagination to try and shut down (black out or, at least, brown out) your secondary fear or fear of fear. Ready to give it a try?

Imagine your body as an immense power plant. It is pulsing with power and generating millions of kilowatts. You are filled with generators, turbines, and engines—even windmills if you like. Your nervous system is a network of high voltage lines through which hundreds of thousands of volts travel. Each hair on your body is a pole with a transformer. Listen to the warm hum of electricity coursing through you. Feel its prickly sensation, almost like ants crawling over the contours of your body. The electricity will continue to flow and hum as long as your finger is on the master button. Your finger pressing down on the button keeps the fire dancing. Use your imagination to decide upon the button's color, size, and location. How much pressure are you applying to it?

If you remove your finger, the plant will not shut down. Rather, its output will drop. There will be a reduction in that prickly sensation.

Go ahead.

Give it a try. Remove your finger and drop your output.

You might try another approach as well. Give your imagination free play. Imagine yourself walking along an open stretch of road. Go ahead. Make it anywhere you like and add whatever scenery you like. The only requirement is that your road, at some point, must wind down into a valley. You have to go down, at least, for a while. As you enter the valley, a sign announces that you are entering the valley of your fear. That sign might read "Boss Valley" or "Airplane Valley" or "Sickness Valley" or even "Loneliness Valley." Can you make out the words written there? If not, you need to write the words on the sign yourself. When you can read them clearly, start your trek through the valley. As you go, remember that you do not enter the valley alone. Read or quote Psalm 23, replacing "death" with the name of your fear: "Yea, though I walk through the valley of _______, I will fear no evil: for thou art with me."

6

A Loose Tongue

Gossip

The French language makes just about everything sound good. Take, for example, the word *gossip, oui-dire* (rendered "hearsay"). In other countries, however, more descriptive terms are used. In Australia the gossip is termed a *stickybeak*. In Scotland gossip is called *clishmaclaver*. But good old Americanese provides the most picturesque term for the gossip: *blabbermouth*.

I have never had a counselee describe his problem with words by saying, "I am a blabbermouth!" or "I have a stickybeak, and it's causing me problems!" I have heard, on the other hand, many people confess that they are blessed with the "gift of gab." "Gift," mind you! If you are a gossip (And here's the dilemma: if you are, chances are you'll never admit to it; rather, you merely "report" the local news!), you are faced with a situation more difficult than containing a raging forest fire or domesticating a wild, raging tiger; you must tame your own tongue! (Jas. 3:1-12).

The most difficult thing about dealing with a loose tongue is recognizing its looseness. Are you a gossiper? You can answer that question by taking the following quiz:

1. When you hear bad news about somebody, you never turn to the same one or two people in order to pass the news along. (True or False)

2. It helps the person in question (the one in trouble) for you to pass on the juicy tidbit about her. (True or False)

3. You never talk on the telephone long enough that you have to switch ears because of "receiver stress" (perhaps the origin of the term *bend one's ear*). (True or False)

4. At your coffee breaks you talk only about positive, upbeat things and never about anybody outside the group. (True or False)

If you answered "False" to at least three of the questions, you may have a raging fire in your mouth or your tongue may be a poisonous dart. You had better see to it right away. As a Christian, you may be using your tongue to praise God one moment and to speak evil of your fellowman or -woman the next (Jas. 3:9).

If you suspect this might be the case (and there's a lot of closet gossips out there!), go before a mirror and open your mouth as wide as possible. Roll your tongue around in your mouth, looking at yourself all the while. Do this for about five minutes. I know of no one who looks good with his or her mouth wide open and tongue rolling around. (As a matter of fact, the tongue is quite ugly, which, is all the more reason to tighten it up and keep it from jumping around.) And while you are standing there in this unbecoming pose, imagine being spoon-fed garbage (coffee grounds, egg shells, potatoe peelings, moldy bread, chicken bones, and yesterday's zucchini). Try to imagine the texture and taste. There is a sense in which gossipers do just this: they take in bad news ("garbage") and digest it without picking out the truth. In this regard, gossiping and lying are first cousins! Another thing you will notice about this exercise is that it causes pain and stress. The human mouth and tongue were never intended to be wide open and flapping like a shutter in a gale for extended periods of time. The mouth looks better closed!

You may not be a gossip, but perhaps you talk too much. Your presence is like Moses' rod. When people see you coming, they part like the Red Sea. You presume on their time and attention with your endless chatter and poor stewardship of speech. Your two ears lay wasted, and your mouth is a great belching sweatshop that ought to be ticketed for noise pollution. Why not cease your long-windedness and listen to the wind for a change?

Try this exercise.

At your home, go outside and sit on the steps or in a lawn chair. Close your eyes and relax. Take the time to rid your system of any pockets of tension or tightness. Now put your two ears (as opposed to your one mouth) to work. Hear what you can hear. Listen to the variety of God's creation. Count the sounds which point to God's creatorship. Perhaps one will be the gentle rustling of the breeze over grass. (Admit it! It's so much more peaceful than your long-windedness!) Maybe you will hear an irate mockingbird in a tree or a cicada. Maybe in the distance you will hear children at play or the sounds of traffic on a nearby street. Count the sounds, the God sounds. You may hear one you have never heard before. It is muffled, like falling snow, and it uses the blood coursing through your veins and your heartbeat as a point of contact. It is called *silence,* and men and women of old often found God waiting there.

And the next time you are with people, don't forget this exercise and return to your longiloquent ways. Rather, continue to listen to God sounds: laughter among friends, the clanking of silverware and dishes at table fellowship, expressions of concern and caring and, perhaps most important of all, the silent cry for help.

7

When You Are Wound Too Tight

Stress

Tension, stress, and all keyed up;
Strain, tightness, and all wrought up;
Frustration, upset, and agitation;
Nervousness, pressure, and perturbation.
These nouns and adjectives cause our ills
By making mountains out of molehills.

It may not be Robert Frost, thank you, but the poem is true. Ours is a pressure-cooker world. Most of us boil in the pot like big, scalded lobsters and accept sleeplessness, ulcers, tranquilizers, and heart attacks as par for the course. Even Christians, who are supposed to sit loose in the saddle, become conformed to the world in this regard. Ministers of the gospel have one of the poorest track records where heart attacks, high blood pressure, strokes, and stress-related diseases are concerned.

What ever happened to *mellow?* During the decade of the sixties, that was a popular word—

almost a cult word. It meant "I'm untroubled!" or "I'm easygoing!" or "I'm calm!" Today, however, *mellow* seems to have given way to *uptight.* Whereas *mellow* was a subculture word twenty years ago, *uptight* is the ritual word of middle- and upper-class respectability. *Mellow* shambled along in bell-bottom jeans, paisley prints, and long hair; *uptight* whirls in dressed in three-piece suits, white shirts, carrying a briefcase. Uptightness is in! And it is downright respectable.

Such respectability is unfortunate, especially for the Christian. Instead of being Christian zephyrs, we come across as human twisters or hurricanes. We are pent up with negative forces. We lack the gift of discernment, the insight to know which things are important and which only seem important. The center of our being is so tightly wrapped with howling, destructive winds that we are capable of blowing the roof off at a moment's notice. More than a few of us are fearful of the word *snap!*

This is not to say that life does not have built-in stresses. Certainly it does. Death, divorce, illness, retirement, business loss, and injury are just a few of the stresses. Job, in the Old Testament, recognized that "man is born to trouble as the sparks fly upward" (5:7). Yet, the chronic struggle—to do more in less time, to drive the wonderful machine you are unmercifully and make yourself impatient and hostile, to set more and tighter deadlines—can be mastered. If you remain in your pressure-cooker world, you may find some secondary effects tagging along with your stress, such as overeating, smoking, drinking, or drug dependency.

You can work on your stress level by paying attention to the exercises in this book. By taking time to exercise your imagination, by being still and quiet and by unloading some of your psychic baggage, you will produce immediate, desirable changes in your breathing and heartbeat and probably in your blood pressure as well.

Trying to discover why you push yourself as you do is a good idea. What motivates you to overwork, to try to accomplish too much, to make more money, or to take on more responsibility? I find that many Christians place themselves under undue stress because they have a "works" mentality. They understand their self-worth to be inextricably bound to productivity. "The more I produce, the better I am." They feel more deserving as a result of their drive and ambition and hardheartedness.

Such individuals are usually short on their understanding of "grace." When grace is defined as "unmerited favor," we cannot earn it no matter how hard we work, how many goals we meet, or how productive we are. Since it is diametrically opposed to human effort, individuals with a "works" orientation are usually heavy into the Protestant work ethic (where a good Christian is characterized by thrift, hard work, and an early-to-bed-early-to-rise mind-set). Thus, you might keep an immaculate house with your obsessive cleaning because it makes you feel inherently superior to (and more deserving than) your neighbor who is piled on the couch in her slippers watching "General Hospital." Or, you might stay on the telephone until ten every night making calls to insure your ace salesmanship. Why? Perhaps you like the positive "strokes" people give you as a result of your hard work and business acumen.

Think about why you put so much pressure on your delicate inner workings. When you discover the reason (be honest with yourself), put your imagination to work. Formulate a mental picture of Jesus and the children and put yourself in with the group of kids. (That's right! Imagine yourself as you once were. You weren't always uptight, you know!) Perhaps your mental picture of you as a child will be based upon your earliest recollection and how you remember yourself looking at the time. Perhaps it will be based upon a photograph you have seen. It can be whatever you like. Use your imagination to set the scene, the scene with Jesus and the children.

How many children are present? What do they look like? What ages are they? How are they dressed? What are they doing? What does Jesus look like? What is He doing? What are *you* doing? Remember, this is you before all that adult responsibility, before you ever put your nose to the grindstone, your shoulder to the wheel, and all that other stuff that came with growing up. This is you without all those serious goals and deadlines and the attending stress and tension. Your only goal as a child was to play and be as happy and carefree as possible. Your only deadline was to play as much as you could before darkness fell. This is the rascally you, the sometimes disobedient you, the dirty you, the dependent you, and the undeveloped you. This is the you who might have been prodding a frog with a stick while Jesus was speaking.

When you can see the scene with clarity, imagine Jesus speaking: "Whoever humbles himself like this child, he is the greatest in the kingdom of heaven" (Matt. 18:4).

Imagine that! Jesus found you to be something special long before you started on the road to your ulcer or hypertension. He saw marvels in you before you got mature enough to worry and be tense and fretful. He pointed you out (or a kid like you!) while you were playing in a sand pile, long before you started making mountains out of molehills. He saw something valuable and unique in you before you started working those fourteen-hour days and trying to prove your worth. It is a shame to run down a terrific creation like yourself! God gave you potential, but stress is wearing down that potential. It is eating away at your servanthood and stewardship of life. Resolve to do something about it.

Get comfortable in that favorite place.

Get in touch with your breathing.

Notice if it is fast or slow, deep or shallow. Do not worry about changing your breathing pattern; just notice it.

Take all the time you need. When you are ready, notice any feelings of tension or stress in that marvelously complex, intricately sculptured body of yours. (Perhaps your hands are clenched, or there is lower back pain, a stiff neck, a headache, or a furrowed brow.)

Give that tension or stress a color. What color do you imagine it being?

You may be the walking form of stress. Perhaps your cup "runneth" over with it. Or, there may be pockets of it burrowed in your body. Whatever, you decide.

When you have selected your stress color, think of the most peaceful, relaxing color you can imagine. When that color is decided upon, let it represent the breath of God, the same breath He breathed into man in the beginning.

As you continue to notice your breathing, beginning with your head and facial muscles, each time you breathe out (exhale), take away some of that tense, stressful color. And each time you breathe in (inhale), bring in the breath of God (your peaceful, relaxing color) into your being. Remember, the breath of God is the breath of well-being and purposefulness and calm.

Continue to rid your body of the tense color and substitute it with the relaxing one. Substitute colors anywhere stress is located within your body. After the head and facial muscles have been "bathed" in the breath of God, go to the neck and shoulders, chest, arms and hands, back, groin, legs, feet and toes.

And when you have been renewed and relaxed

by the indwelling breath of your Creator, meditate upon these words:

"The Lord God formed man of the dust of the ground, and breathed into his nostrils the breath of life; and man became a living soul" (Gen. 2:7, KJV).

8

When You Blow Your Top

Anger

"So Cain was very angry . . ."

Then follows a story whose tragedy is an archetype. With his anger out of control, destructive, Cain slew Abel. We do not know exactly why Cain was so angry. We can speculate, but the story leaves us without a sure answer. What it does tell us in a stark, forthright way is that man, from the beginning, has sometimes let his anger get the best of him.

The Bible does not say that anger is a sin. As a matter of fact, it is a natural emotion and necessary for survival. You might as well wish the tires on your automobile were held in place with toothpicks rather than lug nuts as to wish you had no potential for anger. The lug nuts serve a purpose, and so does anger. Anger is a troublesome fact of life. It is referred to as a negative emotion. It can be as mild as an annoyance (the gnat dancing in front of your face and using your eyelids as trampolines) or as intense as rage (at the joker who runs the stop sign and plows into your automobile).

Jesus, the God-man, exhibited anger. He created quite a scene when His anger became the force by which the Temple was momentarily cleansed (John 2:13-16). Some "church" furniture even got turned over in the scuffling! He was frequently angered by the misguided religious zeal of the Pharisees (Mark 3:1-5). But Paul's letter to the Ephesians sets forth the admissibility of anger in unmistakable fashion: "Be angry but do not sin" (4:26). Apparently it is possible to be angry without being a Cain. The latter part of the verse tells us how: "Do not let the sun go down on your anger." That is, the longer you toy with your anger, the longer you seethe, the greater the potential for destructive use of this emotion. Recognize it, deal with it, and come to grips with it. The poet William Blake penned the two options for dealing with anger:

> I was angry with my friend:
> I told my wrath, my wrath did end.
> I was angry with my foe:
> I told it not, my wrath did grow.

You are faced with quite an obstacle if your anger is on a short fuse. I am referring to people who are happy go lucky most of the time, but suddenly blow their top for no apparent reason. (It's common to hear people who exhibit this trait referred to as a Jekyll-and-Hyde personality.) Maybe you go as far as throwing things, cursing people, even physically attacking somebody. If you have been doing this any length of time, you may have already been introduced to the local constabulary. If not, you probably will given time. Anger that explodes is potentially destructive and requires immediate attention.

The first step in controlling your anger is to be sure the explosions are not triggered by a substance like alcohol. If such is not the case, you need to have a thorough physical examination and rule out a neurological basis for your fits of anger. If you get a clean bill of health, it is time to work on yourself. Let us consider the problem from the standpoint of long- and short-term resolution.

You need to get to the basis of your anger. You will never be able to deal with it until you understand its source. Please! Please! Don't fall into that old deterministic trap which concludes, "That's just the way I am!" There is a reason for your angry reaction. Perhaps it is low self-esteem, a misguided sense of justice (you like to play God), or a life-style built on impulsiveness or frustration. Whatever it is, you are responding in a destructive way to what you consider threat. To find out why your reaction is exaggerated, start a journal (your own personal "anger" book) in which you record your fits of anger. Make notations concerning the time, place, the person or people involved, the circumstances, and what produced the big blowout. Jot down what you were thinking or feeling at the time your fuse was lit. Keep this journal for six months or so (you'll have to be highly motivated to work on yourself to go to that much trouble!), review it and see what it is that tends to bring you to the boiling point so quickly. Once you understand why you get so fighting mad, avoid situations that bring that particular stress to bear. Avoid it, that is, until you are better able to handle the emotion.

But your more immediate need will be something to do during that split second between the time your fuse gets lit and you blow your top. Whoever came up with the idea of counting to ten before unleashing pent-up anger was on the mark. That is an easy programming gesture which momentarily deflects the spearhead of anger from skewering the angry person (and perhaps others as well!) and brings a measure of relaxation to a coiled body.

As a Christian, however, you can improve on the old counting-to-ten method. Memorize three or four Scripture verses and rehearse these in your mind when you feel anger about to erupt. "Love your neighbor as yourself" (Matt. 19:19). "Vengeance is mine; I will repay, saith the Lord" (Rom. 12:19). "Good sense makes a man slow to anger" (Prov. 19:11). There are plenty of choice verses and appropriate phrases to be used to your benefit as a Christian. Self-mastery is a hallmark of the Christian faith (Phil. 4:11-13), and it is time it was one of yours where anger is concerned.

Try this exercise of the imagination.

Meditate upon the words of Ephesians 6:10-17 where we are urged to "put on the whole armor of God." The picture drawn for us is one of loins girded with truth, a breastplate of righteousness, feet shod with the gospel of peace, the shield of faith, the helmet of salvation, and the sword of the Spirit. Take the time to imagine your equipping yourself in armor like this. Put it on piece by piece. Make sure that every piece is perfectly fitted to you.

Sense your invincibility within the armor. Feel its weight.

Concentrate upon this mental picture of yourself (a Christian warrior) for a couple of minutes. Keep looking at yourself until you are certain you are completely covered and protected from all possible harm. Feel free to adjust your protection to ensure your security.

When you are certain no fiery darts can get through to you, remember that nothing outside the armor can hurt you. But your anger is on the inside with you! It is in you! And if you suddenly reached your boiling point and blew your top, you might get angry enough to throw the sword of the Spirit at somebody or something. You could get to shaking so that you drop the shield of faith. You might remove the helmet of salvation to insure that your curses are heard. Not a pretty picture, is it?

Set to work on your anger, keeping in mind that you can be angry. After all, it is a part of you; but you do not have to be a Cain. Do not permit anger to make you a fugitive in the world, a wanderer bearing the mark of hard feelings.

9

A Jaundiced Eye

Prejudice

What do you do when a seventyish pillar of the church—a Bible-believing, God-fearing woman; inspirational, enthusiastic, and dedicated; blue hair, neat and trim—walks up and tells you a racial joke in the hallway of the educational building of your church? Do you . . . (It's quiz time!):

1. Laugh.
2. Ignore the punch line and fake a sudden stomachache.
3. Tell her a racial joke in return.
4. Show your disapproval of such bigotry.
5. Pray that the floor will open and swallow you.

There are any number of possibilities. If you do 4, you risk hurting the woman's feelings and embarrassing her and you. Things may never be quite the same between you.

If you do 2, you prove you are able to think fast on your feet, but you have ignored the issue.

If you do *5*, you exhibit a belief in divine intervention, but in a shallow, "magical" way.

You can do *1*, then, when the woman goes off chuckling to herself, do *5*. Some might call that hypocritical. (I ought to know. I've done *1*, then *5* many times before!)

If you do *1* with great gusto, or *1* then *3*, you have the same problem as the sweet, blue-haired lady: You have a great big gaping hole in your personality! At least, that is what Gestalt Psychology posits. Gestalt says that "holes" in your personality and mine hinder our growth and maturity. (Be careful now! You may find this to be the most distasteful section of the book.) You "project" those parts of yourself you do not wish to be aware of onto others.

—lazy
—untrustworthy
—unintelligent
—fickle
—sex crazy
—greedy
—unethical
—idolatrous
—stuffy.

These unbecoming character traits you see in others are part of you. There are a bunch of people like that sharing the same roof. You've gone condo, man!

It is only natural to resist the idea that you are a racist, a snob, a chauvinist, or an anti-Semitic, one-sided individual. (You're merely possessed of certain strong "convictions." Right?) The test as to whether you are prejudiced or not is simple. How angry do you get when you hear the word *black, Jew, poor, homemaker, Baptist, hippie, working mother, feminist, Republican,* or *divorcee?* Let us say you dislike rutabagas. If I ask you to name your least favorite food and why, you could tell me about rutabagas without your blood pressure rising. But not so with a prejudice. Your voice rises, your eyes narrow, your heart pounds. Usually there follows a flood of generalities learned in the family of origin and accepted uncritically as fact.

"A woman's place is in the home."

"The Democrats (or Republicans) are ruining America."

"Preachers like fried chicken."

"Catholics always play bingo."

"Baptists don't have any fun."

In ancient Athens Paul once addressed a learned audience and told them that God "made *from one* every nation of men to live on all the face of the earth" (Acts 17:26, author's italics). The implication is that the human race, in spite of its diversity, is unified through a genealogy that goes back to our Father, God. Red and yellow, black and white are from the same family stock. With that in mind, it is understandable that God has no favorites (Acts 10:34).

What is important for you to understand is that you were not born with your particular prejudice(s). You were "contaminated" most likely by your parents or other authority figures who expressed their bigotry in what appeared to you, a child, as gospel truth. Now, as a Christian, you need to rid yourself of your prejudice and be obedient to the command to love your neighbor. That contamination makes the words of 1 John weigh heavily upon a jaundiced eye: "If any one says, 'I love God,'" and hates his brother, he is a liar; for he who does not love his brother whom he has seen, cannot love God whom he has not seen" (4:20).

Try this.

Few Christians have not seen a copy or picture of Leonardo da Vinci's famous painting *The Last Supper.* Imagine that painting as you remember it, or, if you have a print, meditate upon it. Visualize Christ and the disciples at table, a kind of family portrait. When you can see this clearly and after adding any details you desire, put yourself in the picture. You can either join the crowd or substitute yourself for your favorite disciple. Imagine what it is like for you to be there, you as you are at this moment.

When you can see yourself and you are seated and comfortable in this "family," one by one bring in some of your prejudices. Maybe it is a black, a Vietnamese, a businesswoman, a Catholic, a food-stamp recipient, a wealthy person, a policeman, whatever. Get each of them seated and, one by one, imagine yourself in their shoes. You become each one! What is it like to be black or a woman or poor at the table with Jesus (a Jew!)? More importantly, what kind of reaction does Jesus have toward you in each pair of shoes? Do you feel any bigotry on His part? Do you sense that He feels any different toward you because you are male as opposed to female, black as opposed to white, poor as opposed to rich, uneducated as opposed to educated?

As you become your particular prejudice, sitting there at table in her shoes, explain to Jesus your concerns and deepest desires. Tell Him your needs as a person, what makes you productive and contented and what makes you dissatisfied and empty. Are these any different from yours (I mean, when you are in your own shoes)? When you have said all you want to say, imagine Jesus speaking to you. (Don't forget. You're still in the shoes of your number one prejudice.) Is Jesus any less enthusiastic toward you because you are a different color, sex, or social class? Or is His message about the kingdom of God, salvation, the Christian ethic, and God's love the same as it has always been?

When you get back into your own shoes, when this exercise in imagination is over, remember how opinionated and critical parental judgments can be. Such opinions deal with everything from religion to politics to family roles to dress. Many of these are not factual. You are a Christian, one who, in Paul's favorite two-word formula, is "in Christ." That means you relive the experiences of Jesus. You experience in your life the same ups and downs, highs and lows, that Jesus encountered during His earthly life. You have a personal identity with Him! He met a variety of men and women representing different blood lines. He met representatives of all social and religious classes in His society. He met crazy people, sick people, "sin-full" people, governmental and denominational leaders. Yet, such classifications never caused Him to desert His message, a message crystallized in John 3:16.

"In Christ" you must work on your jaundiced eye. You may have to sit at the table with the Master again and again to overcome your prejudice. You may have to practice walking in other shoes many times. In fact, it may be a lifetime effort on your part. But as you practice maintenance on yourself, and as you get to know the repressed, bestial parts of your own being, allow yourself to be overwhelmed that God could love one such as you.

10

When You Are Down in the Mouth

Self-Pity

Ask yourself a personal question: For whom do I feel pity? Possible answers include: children who do not receive a visit from Santa on Christmas; the starving masses in Asia and Africa; for the guy down the street who lost his job; the skid-row bum; the football team that just lost its twentieth straight game; old people, the sick, the homeless, and the penniless; the *unfortunate.*

Now, ask yourself, Whom do I want to pity me? Answer: nobody!

The reason we do not want to be pitied is that such human feelings involve a superior-inferior relationship. The one who has pity is somehow considered to be in a position of strength. The one pitied, however, is powerless or helpless. Such is the relationship of God to humanity portrayed in the Bible. For example, in Joel 2:18 we are told the Lord "had pity on his people." Certainly they were in a pitiful situation. They were in the midst of a locust plague. Giant swarms of crawling, prickly legged, vibrating-winged, greedy grasshoppers were eating everything in sight. But God's pity was active, a response calculated to relieve the plight of the people. Through the prophet the Lord promised to deliver the people and land if the former would repent of their sins.

Where people are concerned, however, human pity often involves an element of boastfulness. For that reason, synonyms like *kindliness, softheartedness, compassion, sympathy,* and *tenderness* don't contain that peculiar notion. I might consider the hobo picking through the garbage can pitiful, yet take pleasure in his stumbling, bumbling ways. Such feelings will probably not motivate me to buy him a meal or change of clothes. If, on the other hand, I have *sympathy* or *compassion* for him, I might try to meet some of his needs.

As you can see, pity is not necessarily a redemptive feeling. It is not nearly as apt to draw near to help as, say, compassion. Thus, since much of pity is disrespectful, contemptful, or patronizing, most of us don't want it directed our way. So why does *self*-pity (*poorus meus*) feel so good?

It does feel good, doesn't it? If you have wallowed in it a while, you know. Consider the prophet Elijah in 1 Kings 19. After routing the prophets of Baal in a showdown on Mount Carmel, he aroused the wrath of Queen Jezebel, herself a zealous missionary for Baal. She let Elijah know in no uncertain terms that she intended to put an end to his life and prophetic ways. Forced to flee to the desert, the great man of God appears to be a mess

(vv. 4-8). He sat down under a shrub and asked to die. He lay down and slept, no doubt depressed about his bad luck (a key ingredient in self-pity). Then, a little later, when the Almighty rebuked him for his self-pitying ways, Elijah claimed he was the only faithful person left (v. 10). Enter the second building block of self-pity: Blame somebody (everybody) for the problem.

Had this prophet not been instructed by the Lord to get on with the business at hand (and he was), had he stayed in the desert brooding, he could have collected injustices and bad breaks like baseball cards or doorknobs. These would have freed him from personal blame or responsibility for his plight. You see, self-pity has certain advantages.

Yet pity remains a high-handed, pretentious feeling. The person who is prone to self-pity (and we all like to practice a little *poorus meus* from time to time!) is actually directing this condescending feeling toward a weak, subservient part of the self. For example, "Poor me, they're always putting too much work on me!" might be pity for that "schnooky" part of myself of which advantage is always taken, which is unable to speak up or which I dislike for impotent, helpless ways. "Poor me, nobody knows what I've been through!" might be pity for that faithless, mournful, and moaning lamenter in me who is incapable of overcoming crises and problems and moving on. Elijah's "Poor me, I want to die!" was pity directed in part to that

cowardly part of himself which ran from a foe—
and a woman at that!

You get the picture, I think. Prolonged or persistent self-pity is bad for everybody, especially a Christian. After all, Jesus said kingdom people should be anything but self-pitying.

> "Blessed are those who are persecuted for righteousness' sake, for theirs is the kingdom of heaven" (Matt. 5:10).

> "For whoever would save his life will lose it, and whoever loses his life for my sake will find it" (Matt. 16:25).

Here is another truth about self-pity. If you practice it, you will probably find that difficult to admit. You know, you have had all that bad luck (things beyond your control) or other people have kept you beaten down (It's their fault.) or the Creator didn't endow you with the same endowments He gave everybody else (You have a wooden leg.). Because it's hard to admit to self-pity, *poorus meus* is a monumental obstacle to overcome. If you can admit it, however, you can cease your scornful attitude toward that neglected part of yourself.

Step one is to isolate that part of yourself toward which you are cool, unfriendly, or remote. Make no mistake about it, that may take some time. You may have to do soul searching for days, perhaps monitor your down-in-the-mouth ways for weeks in order to discover that elusive part of you over which the locusts have been crawling (who knows for how long?) unchecked.

When you do make the discovery (By the way,

only the person who is highly motivated to change self-defeating ways will search for this neglected part of himself. Self-pity, like fly paper, has too strong an attraction for most.), it's the time to spring into action. In your quiet place, meditate upon the words of Christ given in response to a lawyer's question regarding which is the greatest commandment.

> "You shall love the Lord your God with all your heart, and with all your soul, and with all your mind. This is the great and first commandment. And a second is like it, You shall love your neighbor as yourself" (Matt. 22: 37-39).

"Love your neighbor as yourself." As a counselor, I can vouch for the reasonableness and practicality of that statement. I see it in action all the time. People who are lacking in self-regard, who are self-abusive, self-destructive, *and* self-pitying usually exhibit little or no charity toward the human race. Likewise, those who possess self-love, who have regard for themselves, interest in where they are going and values and convictions by which they live seem able to relate to their neighbors productively and creatively.

Again, meditate upon the words of Christ and begin to understand how that part of you which has been soaking in the bitter brine of pity is without the grace of God. Understand how your relationship to your neighbor, the esteem in which you hold her, your respect and regard for others, is determined by the degree of wholeness and completeness, or lack of it, found in you. If self-pity is a way of life for you, you can be sure a part of you is standing outside your circle of self-love.

So come on now! Bring in the prodigal. Go in search of that lost sheep. Do so in this way.

Using your imagination, place yourself in the open countryside. (You are about to reenact a story recorded in Mark 5 and Luke 8!) As always, you supply the scenic details. Jesus is not there—you are. As a person "in Christ," you share a sense of identity with the Master, so you will be able to do what is necessary in this instance. You are about to encounter perhaps the most pitiable individual in the Bible. This fellow is insane, naked, living among the tombs, and driven endlessly and restlessly by taunting voices within. He lacerates his flesh and breaks the chains with which men would bind him. Wrapped in the vapors of madness, his problems are legion.

Give your imagination full play. Make sure you can see yourself and the imagined surroundings as clearly as possible. When you meet this poor fellow (He's pitiful!), how do you imagine him looking? Perhaps you are shocked by his nakedness. Perhaps he is hairy, a veritable woolly bear. Or dirty, babbling, threatening, and crude. Perhaps he barks like a dog or walks on all fours. Maybe he curses you. (Make sure you can see this poor fellow in all his dreadfulness clearly in your mind's eye.)

When you get over the initial shock of seeing this crazy person, note that there is something familiar about him. Know what it is? He is that neglected part of you, that part of you kept at a distance, pitied, yet held in scorn! This is the part of the *I* which is you that feeds on pity and nothing else. No wonder he's such a mess!

This may be the helpless part of you, the one people impose upon and of which they take advantage. This is the "schnook" in you, the one who hides behind a tombstone and mourns, "Poor me, I can't help myself." Or it's that part of you which leans apathetically against a tombstone and says, "I'm not responsible. I have the worst luck in the world!" Or maybe it's that part which, digging its own grave as it speaks, says weepily, "Life's been harder on me than anyone else." You see, the possible scenarios are endless.

In the original story, the Master cast out all the disparate, self-destructive demons in this man. Jesus expelled them. The fellow was restored to his right mind. Such is your goal. You must bring the poor wandering part of yourself into the circle of God's love. You must infuse that part with grace and cease treating it high-handedly.

Imagine putting your arms around this wildman. (Ugh!) Go ahead. Permit the love of God to wash over him. With compassion, not disgust, welcome this part of yourself back. Restore it to its rightful place and rejoice in your wholeness. You will become more Christlike. Your self-love and self-respect will increase. Your neighbors, who have had to listen to your moaning and groaning, who have been the objects of your criticism and lack of charity, will rejoice in your completeness. They might even breathe a sigh of relief!

11

Slumped Shoulders

Spiritual Depression

Remember the story of Atlas in Greek mythology? He was one of a group of gods called Titans who fought a war against Zeus. The war was unsuccessful. As punishment, Zeus decreed that Atlas support the sky on his shoulders forever.

Imagine Atlas writing a book on *The Joys of Sky Support.* From there he hits the banquet circuit and makes personal appearances speaking on such topics as "Successful Sky Support," "Getting the Most from Sky Support," and "You and the Sky: A Meaningful Relationship." Yet, look at old Atlas. His shoulders are slumped, his face is contorted with pain and strain, his knees tremble, his arms quiver, and his brow is sweaty. His body language is sending a message other than that of joyous sky support and a positive relationship to the heavens. He will be hard pressed to convince anyone he is enjoying what he is doing.

Likewise, projecting a positive Christian witness is hard when all people read in you is misery, morbidity, depression, and sadness. Your words may be those of peace, joy, and blessedness, but your gloomy countenance will not support your contention. Nobody is going to want what you possess!

Spiritual depression is the inability to experience Christian joy and make the most of one's Christian experience. It is, at heart, a poor stewardship of life, talents, potential, and ministry. It is the antithesis of the biblical admonition to make a joyful noise (Ps. 100:1).

I see a great many dedicated Christians who are active in their churches and faithful in the things of holy living, whose spiritual life is beset by something akin to what the prophet Haggai observed:

> "You have sown much, and harvested little; you eat, but you never have enough; you drink, but you never have your fill; you clothe yourselves, but no one is warm; and he who earns wages earns wages to put them into a bag with holes" (1:6).

Folk suffering from spiritual depression seem incapable of containing joy. Their beings are porous and sievelike. If they could be filled with joy, it would disappear in no time. My experience is that such individuals usually end up doing what Jesus described as "straining out a gnat and swallowing a camel!" (Matt. 23:24). That is, they worry and fret and depress themselves over picayune matters of the Christian life and neglect the fact that their character and behavior are the most unchristian of all.

Spiritual depression originates, I think, from

three sources. The first source is personality patterns. Certain individuals seem predisposed to depression as a result of their developmental history and early life in the family of origin. This factor, the most deterministic of the three, coincides with the old Jewish maxim, "The fathers have eaten sour grapes, and the children's teeth are set on edge" (Jer. 31:29). Because of genetics or personality, these folks experience melancholy and feelings of hopelessness. For example, the individual who develops as a dependent personality is a high risk for depression. Such a person is always fearful of being separated from a loved one or not having that person's approval. Dependent personalities are usually low in self-esteem and high in feelings of guilt. They are clinging vines who avoid anger and conflict lest they lose the love so badly needed. Thus, a dependent personality may suffer depression as a result of a death or separation, as a result of feelings of helplessness and hopelessness, or aggression and anger turned inward. There is no doubt about it: One's personality pattern colors one's religious experience.

A second source of spiritual depression is theology. A great many Christians, while saved by *grace*, apparently do not understand what *grace* means. For them it is so much chatter or holy talk. Many are still plagued by the specter of "law" and their inability to achieve something resembling perfection. They cannot rid themselves of the shadow within, the "old self" (Rom. 6:6), the "first man" (1 Cor. 15:45-48). Every failure plunges them into despair over the fact that "I'm just no good!" (Imagine what happens if your personality pattern is loaded on the depressive side and is compounded by the fact that your personal theology is like the little engine who could, always huffing and puffing, "I gotta make it; it's up to me. C'mon, I can do it, I know I can!" That is apt to get pretty discouraging, that is, unless you are blind to your faults!) To allow oneself to be overwhelmed by grace, to know that you cannot earn merit badges toward salvation, is not easy. Apart from the decision to accept, salvation is all on God's side.

The third factor is akin to the second. I refer to it as the "Thomas syndrome," named for the doubting apostle (John 20:24-25). This particular source of depression refers to the drag or pull of unbelief in our lives. As I see it, unbelief might be the source of all depression. Carl Gustav Jung (1875-1961), the Swiss psychiatrist, noted the role of religious belief in personal well-being. Not one of his patients who were over thirty-five had a problem that was not related to finding a religious outlook on life.[1] If one knew unequivocally (and conclusively, definitively, and categorically) that, as Augustine said in the fourth century, we are made for God and we are restless until we rest in Him, one would not waste a lifetime in empty pursuits.

Whatever the source of your depression and whether you call it spiritual depression, the spiritual "blues" or something else, it is not a pleasant experience. Your spiritual sadness may (and probably does) carry with it the same symptoms of ordinary depression to one degree or another. Your loss of appetite, concentration, and sleep, your sadness, fear, and self-reproach are difficult feelings with which to live.

If your spiritual depression is a matter of "theology," you are fortunate in that it can be easily remedied. Bible study, a good commentary, a wise Christian friend or pastor, the sharing and caring of the saints in fellowship all provide a test of reality for your viewpoints on you, God, church, sin and salvation and sources of information and insight on the same. If, on the other hand, your depression arises from your temperament or unbelief, those are different matters. After years of observing human nature as a counselor and pastor (and being a human being myself for thirty-eight years), my views of determinism are a little Calvinistic. If you have been walking with slumped shoulders all your life, you will find standing straight difficult. And unbelief is that thorn in the flesh of which we never fully rid ourselves. At best we are like the father of the epileptic child Jesus healed. The man cried out, "I believe; help my unbelief!" (Mark 9:24).

You must do something to retain your Christian joy and break out of that horrible religious pucker. As a people-mechanic working on the most important model around, you (No false modesty or religious outrage please! After all, the Father is ultimately holding you responsible for the stewardship of *you* alone!), try this.

Get in touch with the Book of Job in the Old Testament. Read the book if you are unfamiliar with it. (Forty-two chapters of trials, huh?) Once familiar with the book, try to imagine Job before his ruination. How do you see him in your mind's eye? Tall and straight, clear eyed, bright, energetic, and industrious? When you can see him clearly, and he looks exactly as you want (Come on, get him in focus!), imagine him after. (Note how quickly the "Atlas complex" smites Job. The story says "when [Job's friends] saw him from afar, they did not recognize him" (2:12). Fortunately Job did not begin a homily on "How to Turn Crises to Your Advantage." His friends would have seen through him in an instant!) The Scripture helps our imagination at this point. It says Job was covered in sores from head to toe and was sitting in an ash heap doctoring himself. Now you supply the fine touches to your mental portrait of a thoroughly beaten man. (While your eyes are closed and you seek to bring poor Job into focus, verbalize what you see. For example, "There are bags under his eyes." "His mouth droops.")

When you see the man of the ashes as clearly and in as much detail as possible, imagine his feelings at that moment. Remember, Job was trying to figure out what in the world happened. He owned the Ponderosa one minute and the next everything —even his family, minus a nagging wife—was gone. He cursed the day he was born, lamented life in general, protested God's hostility, reminisced about the past, and desired an audience with the

Almighty. What feelings would Job have had? Are any of them like yours?

One trait you and Job have in common is a proliferation of negative thoughts. Listen to him:

> "Let the day perish wherein I was born" (3:3).
> "Why did I not die at birth" (3:11)?
> "Or why was I not as a hidden untimely death" (3:16)?
> "Why is light given to him that is in misery" (3:20)?
> "O that my vexation were weighed, . . . it would be heavier than the sand of the sea" (6:2-3).

(If you want a real challenge, get an adding machine and tally all of Job's somber thoughts!)

You are like Job in that your depression (anger, helplessness, guilt, whatever) is fed by an underground spring of negative thoughts. We are talking a regular artesian well! These come to you thoughtlessly and automatically. They affect your emotions which, in turn, affect upon your behavior. For example, take the negative thought or false assumption, "A good Christian knows God's perfect will at every moment." That leads you to be anxious, depressed, said, even afraid. As a result, you become discouraged, apathetic, and inactive.

Now do what Job did. String all those negative thoughts together, concentrate them into a span of time (say thirty minutes a day), and air them out. Take the time to do this everyday! Confine your negative thoughts like beady-eyed, little extortioners to the prison of your timetable. Do not permit the little sneaks to run free and spoil any and all activities of the day. If you allow these elusive and negative thoughts to do that, church becomes a torture chamber and the preacher, an executioner. You will become distant and withdrawn from the circle of Christian fellowship. The joy of the Christian life will become a moody experience in misconception.

Yeah, misconception! You have to take time to dredge up those negative thoughts and evaluate them as to their reality or unreality. Test them, turn them over and submit them to reason! Is it reasonable to believe that a Christian knows the perfect will of God every moment? What evidence supports such a contention? Learn to formulate counterpoints to your negative thoughts. "I know enough about the will of God to know that He expects me to serve Him, worship Him, and minister in Jesus' name."

This is not a question of getting happy or pulling oneself up by the bootstraps. Rather, it is a question of laying hold on your God-given right to rejoicing, anxiety-free living, thanksgiving and peace (Phil. 4:4-7), all inner qualities which only you can deny yourself. Come on, master yourself! Concerning those thoughts upon which you are building your life, say them, evaluate them, subject them to reason, and, if unreasonable, find alternatives for them.

Try this exercise.

After your daily time of monitoring slippery negative thoughts, repeat the tension exercise in

Chapter 6. You know, the one where you breathe in the breath of God and breathe out tension and stress. Follow that procedure, breathing in well-being and breathing out the bad stuff. In this case, however, as you inhale, repeat the words of Hebrews 12:12: "Therefore lift your drooping hands and strengthen your weak knees, . . ." lift . . . and strengthen.

NOTE

1. Carl Gustav Jung, *Modern Man in Search of a Soul* (New York: Harcourt Brace Jovanovich, 1933), p. 229.

12

A Tight Fist

Greed

A favorite joke of mine goes like this.

A hobo was passing through the state of Texas and happened upon a funeral. The fellow who had died was an oil tycoon. He had left instructions that he be laid to rest in his solid-gold Cadillac. As the hobo and mourners looked on, the deceased's wish was carried out. The millionaire sat stiff and upright behind the wheel of the big, splendid car as it was lowered by crane into the oversized hole. The hobo, bedraggled and penniless and with a stogie in his mouth, watched the proceedings in awe. As the gold Caddy disappeared into the hole, the hobo was heard to whisper with complete admiration, "Man, that's living!"

Speaking of living and dying, have you considered the way we enter this earthly stage and the way we exit? We enter naked—in a state of nature! At one time, people thought a baby entered the world with a *tabula rasa* mind, a blank tablet or page. Today, however, we know the newborn does not have to wait to be "imprinted." From the moment the egg is fertilized, the little fellow is following instructions on how he should grow. Biological inheritances from the parents (and grandparents) affect the developing child from head to toe, including aptitudes and mental abilities. The environment influences the embryo. He is sensitive to substances in the mother's blood. As a matter of fact, the baby is sensitized to the mother's attitude even before birth. Thus, a baby is not a lump of clay that is born but a *person*. The nakedness emphasizes the importance of personhood.

That same person's grand exit, however, is a different matter. He is dressed in Sunday clothes. (This is an updated version of entombing pharaohs with their treasures and Indian braves with bows and arrows.) Some of the personhood seems to have been covered up or lost in the course of the on-stage drama called Life. The soliloquy of birth, the nakedness, gives way to an extravaganza, a rip-snorting cast of thousands; personhood gets entangled with what we have or wish to have. (By adulthood, the nakedness of birth is looked back upon as a "birthday *suit*".)

Personhood is the most fundamental possession we have. It is the way we behave, think, emote, and organize the world around us. It is what makes us a living soul and unique among other living souls. God in Christ seeks to make an impact upon our personhood (personality). In the "soil" of our person, the seed of the kingdom of God is planted and we experience a change of heart. When that happens, we call Master the one who, during His lifetime, possessed nothing except His personhood (Matt. 8:20). We are fascinated with Him because of that fact.

We have difficulty, however, passing through this world without substituting things for personhood. We learn this early on in childhood. The kid on the block who gets the Shetland pony is apt to assume instant stature in the eyes of playmates. She becomes an important person and enjoys the feeling. Consequently our early years are filled with (yah yah!) "Guess what I got today?" or "Mine's bigger and better than yours!"

As the uncertainty and insecurity of who we are mount, and with them anxieties concerning how much we have on the ball, how lovable we are, how pretty or handsome, or how we stack up against the neighbor across the street, the accumulation of things serves as proof of our self-worth. Yesterday having a Shetland pony made me feel like a somebody. Today having three and a half baths or a set of spiffy wheels makes me feel important. The accumulation of thing helps insulate me against doubts about myself and, ultimately, against the fact of my own mortality.

Jesus talked about a man who thought he would live forever. The man's personhood was submerged in and indistinct from his wealth, land, barns, and crops. He thought the manipulation and control of his possessions would insure forever his place in the sun (Luke 12:16-21). But nobody gets out alive. One night the materialistic man's soul was required of him, like that, in the snap of a finger! This fool (for that's what the story calls him) had to leave all his possessions behind. The conclusion to the story is this: "So is he who lays up treasure for himself, and is not rich toward God."

I would mislead you if I said all the avaricious, tightfisted people are in penthouses and driving (or being buried in) fancy automobiles. Far from it. Some of the greediest, most worldly people are in church. Some of them teach Sunday School classes, hear a hundred and fifty sermons a year, sing in the choir, offer the benediction, and serve in every imaginable church capacity. Yet they have no depth to their spiritual lives. What they possess is a thin coat of pious paint, an overlay of orthodoxy, a facade of faithfulness. They are as transparent as a glazed doughnut. They guzzle the sweet milk of mammon rather than the often bitter cup of Christian sacrifice and personal ministry. They do not know a of philosophy of sufficiency. Their life-style reflects more and more and bigger and better.

Greed is the desire to possess things (from doohickies to thingumadoodles) rather than be possessed by the Creator. The irony of greed is this: The more attention you pay to your possessions, the more time and energy they require, the more your most valuable asset, your personhood, suffers.

Perhaps you have reason to believe that your personhood is being swamped in a sea of mindless, spiritless holdings. Perhaps you have no need for concern. In either case, use your imagination to renew your acquaintance with your personhood.

Imagine yourself as the flower of your choice. (I realize such a mental image might be naamby-pamby to a big tough male. Remember, however, that there are some "tough" flowers. You might be a flowering cactus or a tall sunflower.) You can be any flower you desire, but, whichever you choose, you (it) represent the flower in the Bible about which the following is said:

> As for man, his days are like grass;
>   he flourishes like a flower of the
>   field;
> for the wind passes over it, and it is
>   gone,
>   and its place knows it no more (Ps. 103:15-16).

> Man that is born of a woman
>   is of few days, and full of trouble.
> He comes forth like a flower, and
>   withers (Job 14:1-2).

for

> All flesh is like grass
> and all its glory like the flower of
>   grass.
> The grass withers, and the flower
>   falls (1 Pet. 1:24).

With your flower picked out (maybe you don't know its name, but you can visualize it), note all the details you can. What color are you? How tall are you? What shape are you? Is your fragrance delightful or not? Are your petals open or are you a bud? Are your leaves broad or needlelike? Are you hearty or fragile? Where do you imagine yourself growing: in a garden, along the highway, in a mountain meadow, or deep in the woods?

Imagine each of your petals representing some aspect of your material possessions. For example, one petal might represent all your honors (that PhD, MDiv, or RN; that magna cum laude, or that Man- or Woman-of-the-Year award; that respect and esteem in which you are held by your peers). Another might represent the cultural advantages you have had (world travel, social grace, knowing the "right" people, Ivy League schools, the ballet and opera). Still another might stand for your house, cars, jewelry, wardrobe, stocks and bonds. Pick the material possessions you cherish most, the ones with which your personhood is most entwined, and turn each into a fragile petal.

Imagine the petals falling away one by one. Each falls noiselessly to the ground, settling like spangles. They fall until all that is left is your woody stem. Feel your stem drying and dying, ready to snap like a toy glider in a winter gale. You are dying—but not really. You are returning to the ground from whence you came. You are going back to the beginning, back to the seed from which all the color, shape, and fragrance came. That seed, that kernel or core, makes you the living soul you are. There is where the image of God is imprinted. There is where your real, honest-to-goodness treasure is. This is all you will be allowed to take with you when the silver cord is snapped, the golden bowl broken (Eccl. 12:6).

What does it feel like to be in this embryonic

stage? Sit (or lie down) as still as possible, like a seed buried deep within the soil. Listen to the sound of your breathing and the beating of your heart. Feel the weight of your arms and legs. Does your body feel light or heavy?

Remain motionless, silent, and patient. A seed is like that until the time of growth. What does it feel like to be so small, fragile, and unprotected? What is it like to have your personhood—the quintessence of you—set apart from all those adornments and decorations which have been heaped upon it? How do you like yourself without your possessiveness? (It may be frightening and bewildering, like a weightless experience in space. It is also like being an infant again.)

An infant, from the moment of birth, has certain needs which must be met by the parents. Nourishment, clothing, shelter, love, and respect are among the most important. Concerning our needs as persons, Jesus urged us to watch flowers. "Consider the lilies of the field," he said (Matt. 6:28). They are anxiety free! The fatherhood of God promises us that all our needs will be met when we are faithful. Greed is, in the final analysis, the greatest anxiety of all.

(Go ahead. You can grow back now. Come to full flower again. But by all means, don't forget where the Great Husbandman placed your value. It's in the person *you*—not the things you possess.)

13

A Swelled Head

Pride

Bruce Narcissus, a tall, handsome guy, had plenty of girls interested in him. They loved to see him walk by with his chin raised, his arms swinging, and his legs stiff. He was aware of all this female attention but showed no interest in any admirers. He spent hours a day grooming himself before the mirror. Bruce's marvelously chiseled masculine face was in mint condition. He vowed to do all within his power to keep it that way. He wanted to save that face, if you know what I mean. He was always color coordinated, and his apparel was the latest fashions—designer jeans with French names, shirts with meaningless (yet famous) trademarks sewn over the pockets, and shoes and boots with animal names. He traded cars every year, no problem. After all, he went over his quota annually as a topflight salesman (he hated the job); the bonuses kept rolling in. (He had tax shelters right and left!) Travel was a major part of his job, and he always flew first class. He wore contact lenses and lifts in his shoes. His teeth were capped, and he never bought generic products at the grocery store.

In high school Bruce had lettered in three sports. His coach once remarked that Narcissus hated to lose in the worst way—more so than any kid he had coached. Bruce carried that intensity with him to college, where he became an all-conference split end. He graduated with a degree in business administration. Soon after he was graduated, he got his pilot's license and bought his own plane. In time, he also bought a condo. Yet, he was never too busy to hear his friends' problems and usually had a solution for them. (His minor at State U. had been psychology. When listening to these friends or acquaintances, Bruce always steepled his fingers or leaned back with both hands supporting his head.) Presently Bruce is taking up hot air ballooning and gourmet cooking. He jogs a couple of miles a day and is a vegetarian who is into yoga. In his spare time (!), he is pursuing his MBA. He works on his tan in the summer and, even though he hates skiing, makes a trip to Aspen every winter.

Bruce Narcissus is participating in the great national pasttime of saving face. He has elevated himself to the status of god (a little tin god). He could be called conceited, vain, boastful, smug, and arrogant. Some might say he is stuck on himself or has the big head. But what he really is is *prideful.*

As a child, Bruce might have been insecure about his place in the world. He might have experienced low self-esteem. Perhaps he suffered from a lack of love and attention from his parents or a lack of acceptance by his playmates. In adulthood, he is compensating for what he missed by doing what? Loving himself too much? No, not that. (Not *love* by any means! A person with self-love, a necessary ingredient for Christian discipleship, doesn't need to go around congratulating himself. The person lacking in self-acceptance tries to cover up self-hatred with smug, arrogant, and swelled-head ways.) What Bruce does is *worship* himself. It is the old story from Genesis all over again: I wanna be like God! (see Gen. 3:5). (It is also a violation of the First Commandment.)

Pride says that what I have to offer or say or accomplish—my work, status, skills, and ideas—are greater and more important than anybody else's. Thus, this business of immortalizing one-self has traditionally been considered (at least, by the religious community) the essence of sin and springboard to other rebellious acts. For that reason, pride was placed first in the list of seven deadly sins compiled during the Middle Ages.

The Book of Proverbs contain one oft-quoted pearl of wisdom about pride:

> Pride goes before destruction,
> > and a haughty spirit before a fall.
> It is better to be of a lowly spirit
> > with the poor
> > than to divide the spoil with the
> > proud (16:18-19).

If pride is your problem, you may be dangerously close to a fall. Everything about you may be calculated to notify others that they are standing on holy ground in your presence. But, in reality, you are like a house built on the sand (Matt. 7:24-27). Your fall will be heard in the next county!

Steepling the fingers is a classic gesture of smugness and superiority, a body-language tip-off that says, "I'm something special!" or "I have the upperhand!" Concentrate on a different kind of steepling, the kind learned in childhood. You know, the one where you interlace the fingers of both hands, turn the fingertips inward, toward the palms, raise the index fingers together in a "steeple" and repeat this little ditty: "Here's the church, and here's the steeple, open the door, and here are the people" (at which point the palms are turned upward and fingers wiggled wildly).

Steeple your fingers in such a way that they are the symbolic representation of a church steeple. As you relax and quiet yourself, ridding yourself of all those pockets of tension and stress, concentrate upon the steeple you have formed with your fingers. Do not look at it. Just close your eyes and feel its form. When you are ready, having cleared your mind of as much "stuff" as possible and still focusing the mind's eye on the steeple, see what words you associate with it. Perhaps *up, point, heaven, sharp, one way, God,* and any number of others. When you have made as many associations with "steeple" as possible, concentrate on one which will inevitably come to mind: church.

Now imagine your church fellowship and the people gathered in worship. See as many individuals as possible. Note many details. (If your imagination is strong and capable, you might attempt a mental picture of your congregation on a Sunday morning. If that crowd's too much to envision, try a Sunday night. The crowd will be more manageable, guaranteed! And if that's still too much for a mental picture, a weekday prayer service will suffice. Even the least fertile imaginations ought to be able to formulate a detailed mental image of so few individuals! From the individuals present, including yourself, position each from first to last on the basis of gifts and talents. Place the most gifted individual (in your opinion) at the front of the church, then, in descending order of gifts, the lesser endowed. (You could do the same thing with your club members, classmates and fellow workers.)

Where do you place yourself in this "parade" of the gifted? Are you toward the front with the most gifted and talented—the crackerjacks? Or are you in the back with the lesser—the no-great-shakes? (C'mon, be honest. If you are a gifted person with capabilities and skills, place yourself where you rightly belong. You might even be the head crackerjack! False modesty can be as prideful as flagrant haughtiness.) If you see that you belong at the front of the line, consider the words of Jesus: "Whoever would be first among you must be slave of all" (Mark 10:44).

Apparently true greatness lies not in *saving* face

but in *giving* of oneself in service. That steeple you have formed with your fingers is a reminder that the church (you!) is the servant of God in the world. Rightly directed worship is toward God, and rightly directed service is toward people in God's name. Thus, if you placed yourself at the forefront of the gifted, you must be filled with good works and other acts of Christian sacrifice and devotion. Your greatness is your selflessness.

As you continue to visualize your ordering of the more and lesser gifted, look down the way at those you have placed at the modest end of the line. How many of them have you served or helped, or to how many have you ministered? After all, Christian servanthood places others, as the objects of God's love, above self. Thus, self-worship is lost in self-giving. Right?

When you bring this exercise to a conclusion, and when you have cleared your mind of this exercise, try to imagine one other thing. It will be a challenge to envision this. Try to imagine Jesus steepling His fingers!

14

The Ecclesiatical Blahs

Boredom in Church

There you sit, going through your weekly ritual of facing the great wasteland. You get up early, dress in your best, and drive all that way to experience something akin to watching the Sahara landscape change. Yeah, it's Sunday morning worship again, and you are sitting like a stone in your favorite pew.

Take a look around. What do you see? The preacher is in the pulpit, and . . . yeah, he's wearing the same suit he wore last week. He is saying the same things, too—things like, "It's good to see you in worship on this Lord's day" and "There's a blessing in store for you this morning." Poor guy! He is overexposed as can be. He prays practically every public prayer of the week and is expected to be present every time somebody gets sick, dies, or experiences a crisis. He serves *ex officio* on every standing church committee and is the first person approached when Girl Scout cookies go on sale. He is reliable but certainly not a master pulpitarian. As a matter of fact, of late you have become convinced he is a "Vegematic" preacher—one sermon with a variety of attachments. There is nothing mysterious or awe inspiring about him. You even know how much money he makes. Yes, he is completely approachable. A prophet he ain't!

The choir is honing its skills on the same call to worship again. They will stay at it until they get it right! As usual, Brother Funderburk is singing off key. And the order of worship has been followed for years. Same offering plates, same offertory prayer, same peeling paint along the baseboard, same kids squirming, same everything. What is also the same is the fact you are tired and feel drained, even though you slept soundly the night before. Funny thing about that!

Under these circumstances, you are ill equipped to deliver on the purpose of *worship*. How can you show God's "worth" through boredom and languor? The truth is, you can't! The only miracle you will experience in church this morning is one which took place during Israel's victory over the five kings (Josh. 10): The sun stands still! Your hour of worship is going to seem like an eternity!

Your plight is underscored by certain texts from the Bible. For example Isaiah 6:1 records: "In the year that King Uzziah died I saw the Lord sitting upon a throne, high and lifted up; and his train filled the temple."

Or Ezekiel 1:27-28:

> And upward from what had the appearance of his loins I saw as it were gleaming bronze, like the appearance of fire enclosed round about; and downward from what had the appearance of his loins I saw as it were the appearance of fire, and there was brightness round about him. Like the appearance of the bow that is in the cloud on the day of rain, so was the appearance of the brightness round about.

Or Exodus 24:17: "Now the appearance of the glory of the Lord was like a devouring fire on the top of the mountain in the sight of the people of Israel."

Those verses represent the flip side of your problem. In worship, you can't see a thing! You sit in your pew blind as a bat and bereft of any sense of mystery, revelation, and celebration. Jacob had a dream in which he saw a ladder with angels ascending and descending (Gen. 28); Moses saw a burning bush (Ex. 3); shepherds saw angels (Luke 2); Saul of Tarsus saw a light (Acts 9); and John had a vision in which he saw right into the heavenly throne room (Rev. 4). All you see are peeling paint, squirming kids, and threadbare suits. You are unable to penetrate the curtain of earthly realities, to get behind it and see the interconnectedness between your church's squeaky choir (especially Brother Funderburk!) and the heavenly choir of perfect pitch in Revelation 4:7-11. You don't see your pastor in the tradition of John (Rev. 2—3), urging the church (your church) to "hear what the Spirit says" Seems impossible, huh? Can you see your fellow church members, with all their irritating habits and peccadilloes, a part of the new Jerusalem, that city of redeemed humanity in sacred bond with the Father (Rev. 21:2)? Incredible! Yet, these are the very things worship requires. The reason you are unable to do so, and this holds true in most instances, is because you are not trying!

I once saw a picture in a psychology book. A man was lying down and wearing all kind of weird paraphernalia: goggles, gloves with thick cuffs, and his head was wrapped in a sound deadening device. He was participating in an experiment in sensory deprivation, that is, what happens to a person whose senses are denied stimulation. Figuratively speaking, some people (and I believe this reaches epidemic proportions!) approach the worship experience like that man. They turn off their minds, shut down their senses, and dare anyone to disturb their monotony. These folk (and maybe you are one of them) fail to understand that worship is a person-centered activity. The *whole* person reaches out to commune with God. The mind must be actively involved. If not, eyes will not see, ears will not hear, drama will be missing, and Brother Funderburk's chance of singing in the heavenly choir will seem preposterous. (It is more than coincidence, I think, that the fellow in the sensory deprivation experiment at first slept, then became uncomfortable and restless. Ask any pastor if he has ever witnessed similar happenings to people in his congregation.)

So let us approach this disorder with these facts

in mind. First, the burden of worship is on you, the worshiper. Worship is enhanced by beautiful church interiors, the singing of grand hymns, thoughtful planning, and short, concise sermons! Yet, these in themselves are not determinants of successful worship. Conscious, willful activity determines successful worship. Thinking, feeling, participating, willing oneself to see beyond the curtain of earthly realities—from these worship springs spontaneously and honorably. Second, if you are snoozing on your favorite pew, not listening, not seeing, not imagining, not being moved, not focusing with your whole being, your innate need for worship is not being met. If that is the case, dysfunctional things occur much as they do when one is deprived of food or sleep. Truth is, I have talked with folk who, unable to enter into meaningful worship in their church, manifested physical symptoms of insomnia, stomach problems, headaches, colds, or nagging aches and pains. Don't fool around with this disorder! Begin now to work on your church blahs!

Enter into the hour of worship by repeating to yourself the words of Jesus to the Samaritan woman: "God is spirit, and those who worship him must worship in spirit and truth" (John 4:24). Use this verse (or any other meaningful verse, phrase, or word you choose) as a prelude to communing with the Father. Perhaps you could go to sleep Saturday night repeating it to yourself and meditating on what those words mean. Allow it to prepare you for the day of worship. Or wake up with it as a reminder of what the Lord's day is about. You might choose to repeat it to yourself while driving to church or taking your seat once there. Let its silent recitation serve as an initiation rite or password ushering you into the worship of the true and living God. If people greet you, greet them back, then return to the quiet conversation with your innerself. Time spent this way is so much more productive than swapping recipes or ball scores while waiting for the service to begin!

Make a conscious effort to keep your eyelids from drooping or your eyes from becoming set in a blank stare. (Even when looking directly at the preacher, you will never make him believe you're anything but asleep if your eyes rarely blink! Folk who do so are in a trance sure enough, but not like those the prophets experienced. Rather, theirs is a trance of boredom or indifference.) Do not permit your shoulders to slump or your chin to drop. Arms crossed over your chest is going to make everyone think you are mad at somebody. (It'll scare the poor preacher witless!)

You must begin to *train* your body for worship. Tilt your head toward the speaker (it shows interest) and lean the slightest bit toward him (in other words, you're on the edge of your chair in expectation!). Along with this training of the physical body, keep your senses activated. Don't let them go to sleep! Instead of permitting the mind to fall prey to random images which filter in and out when it's blank, keep it alert and focused. You are involved in something as fundamental to humanity as eating a healthy meal or getting necessary rest. This is worship! Don't expect to meet God with half-opened eyes, your mouth open in a yawn, or your thoughts scattered like leaves in a whirlwind. That will never happen!

Reflect upon what you see, hear, smell, taste, or touch. Your church contains symbols upon which you can concentrate. (That's right! Even Protestant churches have them. As a matter of fact, your church building is a symbol!) The pulpit behind which the preacher stands is a symbol of proclamation. Meditate upon the action which will take place there. What about the baptistry? That is where people give public testimony to their death, burial, and resurrection as followers of Christ. If worship is a baptismal ceremony, listen to the sound of the water as the candidate enters and the sound as the candidate is immersed. It is a long way from the Jordan River to that baptistry, yet the water made the same sound when Jesus was baptized by John. And when you eat the Lord's Supper, do you notice the taste and texture of the bread? What about the fruit of the vine? Do you ever try to envision what the preacher is saying during the sermon? Do you listen to the inflection of his voice? Do you ever notice the weight of the Bible in your hand, the feel of the cover and the pages?

There are countless stimuli upon which to focus. Maybe your church has stained glass windows, a cross, or a banner. Seek for the meaning behind each. Probe, search, investigate! Let each play to your senses, to your imagination, until you can see beyond—until you hear Brother Funderburk's squeaky singing in a new light!

I am persuaded that true worship is one of the most difficult undertakings in life. That's why the ecclesiastical blahs are epidemic. Worship involves discipline; for that reason, some believers don't bother with it. They see it as a passive pursuit, something done to them. The preacher preaches to them, the choir sings to them, public prayers are lifted for them. Just being present as a sanctified lump of flesh is efficacious! Don't believe it for a second. The blahs in worship are dangerous to your health. If you doubt it, try the following exercise in imagination.

Do you remember the story of Eutychus in Acts 20? He was a young man in Troas who, perched in a window while Paul preached, fell asleep, tumbled out, and dropped three stories. Try to imagine how Eutychus must have felt if he woke up half way down!

15

A Bare Face

Lying

There is little wonder that lying was never placed on the list of seven deadly sins. It's just too useful! Sure, Aunt Martha's apple pie tasted like a slab of cardboard! Yet your parents instructed you to say with utter sincerity, "I enjoyed it!" when you finished choking down a slab. Your parents also told you to answer the door and tell the encyclopedia salesman they were vacationing in the Bahamas. After a few years of such conditioning, you learned about the permissibility of "social" lies.

"How do you like my new outfit?" "It's very nice!" (*I wouldn't be caught dead in that!*)

"How about we take a look at those home movies I made at the Grand Canyon last year?" "Sure thing!" (*Not those boring movies again!*)

"What did you think of the sermon Sunday morning, Brother?" "Preacher, it was one of your best!" (*It was dry as dust!*)

"I believe my golf game's improving!" "I believe you're right, Boss!" (*You ought to take up croquet!*)

To tell the complete, raw truth in every instance would be akin to carrying a deadly weapon. Armed in such a way, a person would soon be considered less virtuous and more unfeeling and hardhearted. The truth can be hurtful! For that reason, not only are we conditioned to believe that a certain amount of falsification is normal but downright merciful too. Thus, we become adults with the conviction that the "white lie" is an indispensable social tool.

As we get older, we should have a decreasing need to exaggerate and falsify. Facing up to the way things really are is a mark of maturity. We expect children to resort to lies. Somehow we expect adults to honor the truth. As it happens, however, lying sometimes becomes chronic, a habit we are unable to break or manage. Compulsive lying usually begins in childhood with emotionally conflicted children. Most of us have met such a person who, as an adult, tells a lie when the truth would better serve. There is nothing to be gained by the lie, yet it is second nature to tell it. This is abnormal.

The chronic liars with whom I have contact are nearly always lacking in self-esteem. They tell lies in order to bolster their image of inferior personhood. Lies, in their way of thinking, allow them to present themselves in a better light and shore up sagging worth. The bottom line is this: Chronic liars are lacking in self-respect and self-love.

Holy Scripture speaks with a unified voice against the use of deceit and lies. The law of Moses stated pointedly that "you shall not steal, nor deal falsely, nor lie to one another" (Lev. 19:11). If one used lies for personal gain, one had to make full restitution *plus* add a fifth to it (Lev. 6:1-5)! The Wisdom literature notes that "the Lord abhors . . . deceitful men," (Ps. 5:6) and "the mouths of liars will be stopped" (Ps. 63:11). Proverbs says that one of the six things the Lord hates is "a false witness who breathes out lies" (6:19).

> No man who practices deceit
>   shall dwell in my house;
> no man who utters lies
>   shall continue in my presence (Ps. 101:7).

> A false witness will not go
>   unpunished,
> and he who utters lies will not
>   escape (Prov. 19:5).

When lamenting over Judah, the prophet Jeremiah observed the following:

> They bend their tongue like a bow;
>   falsehood and not truth has grown
>   strong in the land (9:3).
> Every one deceives his neighbor,
>   and no one speaks the truth;
> they have taught their tongues to speak lies (9:5).

And Amos, speaking of judgment on Israel, said "Their lies have led them astray" (2:4*f*). Zephaniah, referring to a righteous remnant left in Israel, said, "They shall do no wrong and utter no lies, nor shall there be found in their mouth a deceitful tongue" (3:13).

Paul wrote these words to one church: "Do not lie to one another, seeing that you have put off the old nature with its practices" (Col. 3:9). Jesus cut straight to the heart of the matter and did so with beautiful simplicity: "Let what you say be simply 'Yes' or 'No' " (Matt. 5:37). What a kingdom person says ought to be believable! No exaggeration, no embellishment, no oaths to back it up and, above all else, no falsifying.

There can be no doubt that where the Bible is concerned lying is not a fit practice among the faithful. The first book of the Bible begins with a lying serpent bringing chaos to perfect order. The last book speaks of Satan deceiving the nations. Chaos again! If you are a chronic liar, you are probably in chaos yourself.

Few things bend as easily as the truth, and few things are harder to cover up. The human body seems to rebel against falsehood and misrepresentation. Few of us (very few!) are Grade A, first-class, whiz-bang liars. Anybody can tell a whopper, but those who can do so without signaling the fact are rare, indeed. About the only thing rarer are those who, with a degree of consistency, are able to consciously spot lies.

Sometimes we are tipped off to lies without being aware of it. The woman who covers her mouth with her hand as she speaks, the man whose face twitches, the child who refuses to look us in the eye, the teenager who swallows too much—

each of these might make us doubt the validity of what is being said. We are not sure why we doubt it—we just do!

Not long ago, I was watching a college basketball game on television. It had been a tight, very intense game, the lead seesawing back and forth. During the postgame interview, the losing coach, in a magnanimous gesture, told the interviewer the better team had won. Immediately, however, his index finger went to his nose and barely brushed it. That is a classic gesture of negation. It was a gesture which said, "Cancel what I just said!" Assuming that the coach's nose was not itching, the gesture made me doubt what he had just told the interviewer. *The better team just lost!* was his true feeling about the game.

Everything about you—facial expression, hands, eyes, shoulders, words, gestures—tends to wave little red flags when you lie. For that reason, few people are really accomplished liars, with the exception of professional con men and sociopathic personalities. The latter are lacking a developed conscious and, as a result, possess little, if any, sense of guilt. You can never be as accomplished at lying as they are! By now, even if you have not met a person who is able to consciously read your body clues and knows you as a—it sounds harsh to say—a liar, plenty of folk probably *suspect* you are one. If asked, they would most likely say it is a "feeling" they have about you. (It's inevitable that they should! You're tipping them off to the fact! You're a house divided: The rest of you is refusing to go along with what your mouth is saying!)

Before you begin to work on discovering or recovering self-esteem, break the lying habit. That is the first step. What you are doing only adds to the self-hatred you feel. The truth will make you free (John 8:32), not lies; truth concerns your good qualities and positive attributes (to which you're blinded!) and the bad and negative (to which you insist others be blinded!). Besides, you have yet to fool God a single time; people sometimes may be fooled, but never God! He sees through your lies and cover-ups. He knows the real you—the one hiding behind all those falsehoods. That is the person He wants to liberate from self-defeating ways and counterfeit living.

Breaking the lying habit will not be an easy thing to do. Somewhere along the way, you went beyond the normal bounds of lying into the excessive. After that, every time you told a lie, you strengthened the tendency to resort to exaggeration, invention, and overstatement. Each lie was like a single fiber being woven into a rope. By now, you have fashioned a rope capable of docking the Queen Mary! Don't expect to break it all at once.

Get comfortable and ready to meditate on a couple of things.

First, Joseph Campbell, the renowned student of world myth, recounts a story about the West African god, Edshu, the trickster. One day Edshu was walking along a path which ran between two fields. In each a farmer was at work, and Edshu had an idea. He put on a hat that was red on one side, white on the other. At the end of the day's work, one farmer said to the other, "Did you see that fellow in the white hat?" The other replied, "The hat was red!" "Wasn't," "was," "wasn't," "was," they argued, finally resorting to blows and nearly killing each other.[1]

Meditate on how your tongue (mouth) is working that kind of chaos in your other body members. It walks along the pathways of your being and practices deception, treachery, and trickery, setting itself against all others. Only none of the other body members are going along with the joke! Your tongue speaks a lie; your eye twitches or looks away, your throat gulps, your hand flies to your face, or your voice sounds funny. They all seem determined not to permit the lying tongue to get away with it.

For me, the story of Edshu is somewhat reminiscent of a cherished story within the Judeo-Christian heritage. A young fellow, a real mama's boy, was named Jacob, "Trickster." He perpetrated a joke based on a lie on his blind father, Isaac. As a result, he stole the paternal blessing meant for his older brother. Read Genesis 27. That lie set in motion a startling chain of events, including a forced departure from home, a dirty trick played on Jacob by his uncle, a wrestling match in the dark, and a tension-filled homecoming.

Second, meditate upon these words from the Letter of James in the New Testament: "For we all make many mistakes, and if any one makes no mistakes in what he says he is a perfect man, able to bridle the whole body also" (3:2). ("Able to bridle the whole body"! That's definitely not you, my friend, since your body members are rebelling against the false pontifications of your tongue. "Perfect" you aren't, and no matter how accomplished you are as a liar, or how many lies you tell, no one's ever gonna believe you are!)

> So the tongue is a little member and boasts of great things. . . .
> And the tongue is a fire. The tongue is an unrighteous world among our members, staining the whole body, setting on fire the cycle of nature, and set on fire by hell. For every kind of beast and bird, of reptile and sea creature, can be tamed and has been tamed by humankind, but no human being can tame the tongue—a restless evil, full of deadly poison (Jas. 5, 6-9).

James's point is in verse 10: "From the same mouth come blessing and cursing." The mouth which today is praising God is tomorrow cursing a neighbor. Inconsistency is the tongue's most dangerous (and best known) characteristic. We might paraphrase James this way: "From the same mouth come the truth and lies."

Try to envision this. Your body is a household where every member witnesses to the truth except the tongue. The tongue is constantly urging the eyes, shoulders, hands—all the body members—to go along with the joke, the trick, the deception. Only, they won't—or can't!

As long as you persist in telling falsehoods, using lies to strengthen your self-image, you will be a divided soul. Your crooked tongue will be at odds with the rest of you. Why? Because the truth is easier to bear. Lying puts you in a strain. (After all, that's what polygraphs pick up on: minute physical changes, like perspiration, caused by lying.) And what could be more stressful than an ongoing battle royale between your tongue and voice, eyes, face, and shoulders?

Go ahead! Call a truce between your warring members. Bring peace to your household.

Get comfortable and do what you did in Chapter 7.

Get in touch with your breathing pattern.

Breathe in the breath of God, breathe out the tension and stress. Some of that tension may have been caused by that tongue of yours!

Begin with your feet and legs and work up. Rid all your members of those feelings of strain and tension. Permit the breath of God to replace it with relaxation and peace. When one part (legs, for example) has been transfused with calm and well-being, consecrate it to the truth. Move on to the next.

When you work your way up to those tiny muscles in your face, give special attention to your tongue. Run this proverb through your mind:

> There is one whose rash words are
> like sword thrusts,
>   but the tongue of the wise brings
>   healing (Prov. 12:18).

Vow to cease stabbing everyone with those lies.

Vow to bring healing—to yourself. Consecrate that "little member," as James called it, to the truth. Then, when you are ready, take your new commitment to the truth out into the world and . . .

Practice,
Practice,
Practice!

NOTE

1. Joseph Campbell, *The Hero with a Thousand Faces* (Princeton, N.J.: Princeton University Press, 1949).

16

Toward a Theology
of Human Maintenance

Meaninglessness

In this book I have addressed you, the reader. You have been told to do all those hard things—like confronting your blind spots and developing your imagination. You have been the one working on various character disorders; you were urged to tune up the wonderful piece of machinery you are and to keep yourself in fine working order. One might suppose I am the answer man, perfectly well adjusted, dispensing advice with the dispassion of a gum-ball machine plunking candy into the chubby hands of children.

Such is not the case. To give equal time to my maintenance needs as opposed to the readers alone, allow me to share out of my experience. What I am about to recount was the greatest spiritual crisis in my life to date. Perhaps—just perhaps—it is every person's great disorder. I have saved it for last in the personal belief that such is the case. I use it as a springboard to developing a theology of human maintenance for us all.

Meaninglessness

The most important decision I ever made took place May 15, 1966, a Sunday. There was much which preceded the decision of that day.

To begin with, I am the product of small-town life. My hometown in rural southwest Alabama was born on the Mobile and Birmingham railroad. Eventually, Northern lumbermen came south to establish a mill in the dense pine forests. That began a relationship which has remained faithful down to the present day. Thus, railroad and sawmill are among my earliest memories.

Next to my family of origin, that town has had the biggest influence on my life. It has made me a regional man, an anachronism in a day of transience, mobility, and change, a venial sin at best in a day of world citizenship. It is not that I do not have universal concerns, for I certainly do. But a regional man tests the flavorfulness of a pie by cutting a sliver rather than attempting to digest the whole. He believes the cook has distributed the taste evenly throughout. For that reason, a regional man believes that to know and be known in a locale is about all one can ask of life. A regional man knows the best fishing holes, the best places to eat or get a good cup of coffee; he knows the fellow on the table at the funeral home and the mother of the child just born. And he remembers things: droughts and floods and fires and unforgettable characters who were themselves regional people. To be a regional man, one does not have to shout slogans or display car tags with bigoted or prejudiced humor. As a matter of fact, a true regional man knows that those of his kind are at every point of the globe. He is content to be identified with his small space, and he senses something bigger in it all—a world contained in a raindrop. And above all, he has a sense of pilgrimage, of passing through, knowing full well that nothing is constant except the space itself.

I have not spent my entire life in my hometown. Distance as much as proximity resulted in what you probably perceive as utopian reverence for my hometown. There have always been plenty of flies in the ointment of a small town. To these I am not blind or ignorant. If what I say seems too maudlin, it is due more to a sense of beholdenness than a lack of objectivity. Simply stated, I am an alumnus of a small, sawmill town; the commencement was unforgettable, a strangely moving experience.

Since my father was a serviceman, we moved many times from my fifth year on. In the late fifties, he was stationed in Germany. We climbed the spires of musty and historic cathedrals, took picnics in the countryside in summer when the sky was full of gliders and went to ice shows during winter. We saw men in lederhosen. We saw the Rhine, the Black Forest, and the *Zugspitze.* We saw the ruins of World War II; the pox of war still scarred cities fifteen years after the disorder ended. We came to appreciate the food, the sauerbraten, the dark bread, and equally dark chocolate, the pastries and veal. It was a life-altering experience for a boy.

We came stateside in 1960. I attended the eighth and ninth grades in my hometown, a rare treat, and the tenth grade at the high school in a neighboring town. In time, my father received orders for Columbia, South Carolina, and we moved. The eleventh grade was not a good year for me. I had no friends, did not try to make any, and thus had no social outlets. Just shortly before we moved back to Alabama, to Birmingham this time, I experienced something one night.

My aunt was flying in to help us move. Her flight was to arrive at a late hour, and my parents drove to the airport to meet her. I was left at home in charge with little to do since my sisters were fast asleep. In order to hear my parents and aunt when they got home, I went to the living room and sat in the recliner. All lights were out in the house, and there was no sound at that late hour except the occasional passing of a car. After a few minutes of experiencing the blackness and silence, a feeling of utter abandonment, a rush of forsakenness, washed over me suddenly. It was a frightening experience, this attack of anxiety which, after a few minutes, I was able to get in hand. I had never before felt such a sense of aloneness, such panic, though I would become intimately acquainted with the feeling over the next few years.

In the twelfth grade, the cycle of self-imposed exile repeated itself. It was born in the toxic atmosphere of constant brooding. Anxiety gripped me and made me feel as if I would be utterly devoured by anonymity, chewed up and swallowed without regard for personhood. It came to grip me in ever-tighter coils. I came to believe the only safe place was at home, where I was known. I would fake illness so I didn't have to enter the dead zone at school, where I felt I was of no more importance and had no more purpose than a slug. I experienced a constant choking sensation and was forever fighting flight and a sense of dread. From that ordeal I think I have some small sense of the terror agoraphobics must feel while walking to the mailbox.

At some point the anxiety ceased to moderate in the presence of family and familiar surroundings. It became what Luther called *anfechtung*, a malady of the spirit, a seething inner cauldron of doubt, panic, desperation, and desolation. What if I were a slug and nothing more in the scheme of things? What if there were no more purpose in being than I was experiencing at that moment? What if there were no God, or, if there were, what if He were as distant to and heedless of my needs as those automatons around me? What if I were locked in solitary confinement in the prison which was me, and what if there were no exit? What if, when all was said and done, life were only emptiness?

At times the struggle filled me with spiritual pride. I felt I had gained some valuable insights and truths from the clashes on the dark banks of the Jabbock which was my soul, blessings wrought in scratching and clawing at a foe best described as the specter of purposelessness. As Jonah might have boasted of an intimate knowledge of whale anatomy, I was filled with a hubris of religious struggle. I had seen the dark side of the moon! I had soul! I had been there! Then, at other times, I was too miserable and doubt ridden to do anything except envy those who were able to accept life as it appeared and did not question whether there was more to it. To this day, matters of faith are a struggle for me, and I still have within me a small battlefield reserved for the clash of purposefulness and emptiness, panic and Psalm 131, calling and torpor.

During my senior year, my father received the orders we had been dreading. He was going to Vietnam. We would be moving back to my hometown where my mother, sisters, and I would await his return. I would spend my last three weeks of high school going through the motions there. My diploma, signifying that I was a bona fide graduate of a big-city high school, would be mailed to me. Thus, in the company of friends I had known all my life and attended school with in grades eight through ten, I closed out a terrible year on a happy note.

That brings me back to May 15, 1966.

While I was not looking forward to graduation exercises, I assumed I would be part of the cap-and-gown coterie at the local high school, even though mine would be an alien diploma. At some point during the week preceding that fateful Sunday, the school principal, responding to my query about cap and gown, informed me in no uncertain terms that I would not be a part of any graduation activities. The news thrilled me to no end! Grade twelve had been a washout, and no amount of pomp was going to alter the circumstances. What was joy to me, however, was disappointment to my mother and other family members. A proud moment, commencement for the son/oldest grandchild, had been denied them. That letdown, coupled with my father's recent departure, cast a gloom over the family.

Under these dispirited circumstances, my family and I sat in the white frame church building that Sunday morning in 1966, the Baptist church situated a few hundred yards from "downtown." (Just across the road from the church were the steel tracks over which, more than once, the din of a passing train drowned out congregational singing or spirited preaching. Just beyond the tracks were the warehouses, sheds, and equipment of the sawmill. The profane mill, like a sprawling bully, dwarfed the tiny white church building, even though the bully was reverent on the Lord's day.) The seniors were in cap and gown in a nearby town, listening to the baccalaureate address delivered by the Baptist preacher there. As we sat in our small congregation, listening to the new and aggressive preacher recently called to the church, my mother sniffed her way through most of the service, and other family members no doubt prayed for divine chastisement for the principal who had denied me (them) a milestone.

The new preacher was friendly and likable, animated in the pulpit, hoarse at the end of each sermon, all unmistakable signs, I thought, of God's hand upon him. On that Sunday morning, I sat engrossed in his delivery. When the invitation hymn was sung, I made my one and only march of graduation week. That was to the front of the church to take the preacher's hand in reconsecration and to weep for reasons I did not fully understand. At that moment, however, on a day I remember as sun soaked and drenched in blue sky, a sense of calling was born in me. What appeared to be a moment of denial, a refusal to allow me to sit with my peers and hear the platitudinous challenge given every graduating class, instead turned out to be a sort of deliverance. When the seniors graduated Friday evening, May 20, 1966, I was elsewhere. I don't remember what I was doing, but no doubt I was basking in the warmth of new possibilities opened to me five days earlier.

By no means did the struggle end. I continued to wrestle with that feeling of emptiness and sometimes despair. I took long walks along roads where, four or five years earlier, I was a carefree boy riding my bicycle. Now I walked along burdened with the weight of the world. If I never seek the truth again, I was a seeker during those years. I struggled to gain a little ground and instantly lost twice that much. I was an erstwhile doubter and skeptic, who wanted to believe more than anything in the world. Out of those years of personal unrest, I learned to appreciate pilgrimage, paradox, and the human condition. I came to realize that if my personal life script, which does not always adhere to the principle that the shortest distance between two points is a straight line, is valid, so might my neighbor's life script, equally as circuitous, have validity. Those few years of trial taught me both to accept my own humanity and not beat up on anyone else because he or she could not be more consistent than I.

My home church licensed me to preach and, within a matter of months, I was given the opportunity to serve there as interim pastor. The preaching must have been hard line, pure grit, and sandpaper because I remember one of the deacons' wives requesting that I soften my approach a little the next Sunday. She was not being uncharitable or unchristian, but she was probably voicing the sentiments of most of the congregation. They were trapped with one of their own, having put the stamp of approval on me by licensure the previous summer. Now they had to listen to a nineteen-year-old parroting what he had always heard as gospel, or thought he had heard, little of which was tempered with experience. I was doing what the certificate of licensure said, exercising my gifts of ministry. The experience was unforgettable for both church and promising young preacher.

Flesh-and-blood saints in that church helped me, a struggling pilgrim in their midst, more than they will ever know. Jim Halford. Joe Bill Fendley. Bernard Faile. J. LE. McNider. Jimmy Linton. Dorothy Fendley and her sister, Clida Lee, were stalwarts in the choir. People like Archie Fendley and Ruth Munn, affirmed me and gave me the confidence to believe that maybe the Almighty had layed a task on me. What those people's lives will mean in their entirety, I would not presume to say. But from 1966 to 1970, they were the church in flesh to me.

An image my mind seizes upon are bright, cold, and blustery Saturday mornings. I, the newly licensed, interim pastor, would go to the freezing church to finish Sunday's sermon. It was hushed inside, the mill sounds far away, or so it seemed. I would light the space heater in the back corner of the auditorium and shiver until the circle of heat managed to dent the surrounding cold. Downcast and dispirited, I would wrestle with the text and pray for guidance—not so much for the sermon's delivery as for a way around my personal despondency. But in the delivery of those sermons I talked to my friends, the church members, about my trials and tribulations. I tried to share what I was learning about God and man (myself). For those who heard them, they were just poorly crafted sermons. But the trembling soul in the pulpit was working his way through a crisis with the help of a few listening ears.

Toward a Theology

In the years since, I have thought much about the crisis I have just described. Whether it was a test sent by the Almighty, a snare set by the evil one, or a rite of passage fired by hormones to force me across the frontier into manhood, I cannot say with certainty. The last possibility seems far too simple, the first most plausible. This much, however, is certain: This upheaval of the spirit, this bloody combat between hope and meaninglessness, was the great trial of my life.

I wish now that I had been better acquainted with the Book of Hebrews during that crisis. Looking back, I can see that I did certain things which that writing advocates. Only I did so by chance, not design. Had that book been in my arsenal of coping devices, I would have been better equipped and more inspired to work on myself.

Hebrews was addressed to Christians who were in danger of losing their grasp on the realities of faith. They were experiencing the "drag" of old, unproductive ways. Some New Testament scholars think the audience addressed was out of a pagan background while others say these were Jewish Christians. Whichever, they were wavering, downhearted, and on the verge of forsaking their newfound faith. They were not on an emotional high (far from it!). They had a minimum amount of inspiration and a maximum amount of cares. Right then, being a Christian was not something which felt good!

For that reason, the author did not try to encourage them with talk about capricious feelings. He was not an advocate of stump jumping! His message is one of holding on against all odds, even when all will power is gone.

> Let us hold fast the confession of our hope without wavering, for he who promised is faithful (10:23).

> For you have need of endurance, so that you may do the will of God and receive what is promised (10:36).

> But we are not of those who shrink back and are destroyed, but of those who have faith and keep their souls (10:39).

> Consider him who endured from sinners such hostility against himself, so that you may not grow weary or fainthearted (12:3).

> It is for discipline that you have to endure (12:7).

> For the moment all discipline seems painful rather than pleasant; later it yields the peaceful fruit of righteousness to those who have been trained by it (12:11).

Hebrews is a hard book in this regard. The book is for folk who are unable to keep up emotionally. It is for those whose fire has gone out, who are running on empty and are bone weary. This is stuff for those who don't feel very Christian! "Keep moving ahead, not because you want to or feel like it, but because you have to do so!" said the author. Set your face and plow ahead, running "with perseverance that race that is set before us" (12:1).

The theology of this book is tailor-made for everything discussed in these pages. Certainly discipline and perseverance are necessary to develop one's imaginative capacities. Beyond the obvious, however, is the impact Hebrews has on our perception of problems and disorders. If you are dealing with a broken heart or fear or anger or a problem with lying, you might feel dejected, defeated, or like a second-class citizen. Not so, says Hebrews. What you actually have is an opportunity to exercise your faith. (Remember the eleventh chapter, the "faith" chapter, is the one most readily identified with Hebrews!)

More importantly, however, the theology of this book confronts us with the way things are in life. This is not a perfect world—no where near it! Circumstances can be trying, downright difficult. During my personal "dark night of the soul," I was troubled by the fact that trial should befall me, that I was struggling and hurting and unable to right myself instantly. Somehow I had been led to believe that a Christian's way is trouble free, effortless (God does everything) and filled with answers, not questions. The whole painful business seemed all wrong! I could have used Hebrews' emphasis on perseverance. I needed somebody to tell me not to wave the white flag of surrender—that what I was experiencing others had experienced too and overcome by faith. I needed that bone-and-gristle gospel crystallized in that marvelous book.

Whatever troubles you, whatever self-defeating habit or disorder makes you less than you can be in Christ, whatever "mechanical" problem you have, deal with it tirelessly and with patience. Do not expect it to be fun or to feel good. Do it because not doing it is like turning away from freedom and to bondage (or, in Hebrews' terminology, turning away from the Promised Land and back to Egypt!).

As you work on yourself, draw on those inner resources. Be as creative and imaginative as possible. Your perseverance, coupled with faith in a loving Heavenly Father, can and will result in your personal refinement. (Hebrews isn't the only book in the New Testament to teach that: James 1:2-4; 1 Peter 1:6-7.)

In the theology of Hebrews, you and I are pilgrims, always on the way and never quite there. As we go, two things are required of us: that we should believe in what we cannot see (sounds a little like imagination, huh?) and that we be possessors of a never-say-die attitude.

I wish you success as you work on the wonderful "machine" which is you!

Epilogue

A Parable
(Extremely Paraphrased)

A certain Christian fellow wanted to sow the seed of Christian imagination in his life.

And as he tried, some of the seed fell by the wayside. They did absolutely nothing except lay there. In time they disappeared without a trace, as if they had been gobbled up by birds and things.

Some of the seed represented halfhearted attempts and, because the sower was lacking in proper motivation, what he imagined was without depth and took no lasting root in his life. The seed barely began growing when they withered away.

Then again, some of the seed of imagination couldn't find nurture in the wasteland which was the sower's life. He was a veritable wilderness of wasted energy, double-mindedness, barren ideas, and purposeless living. The feeling of hopelessness strangled the seed of imagination.

But other seed (by the grace of God!) found their way into the few fertile regions of the sower's life, and these produced astonishing results. I'm not sure about the numbers, but when his imagination started bearing fruit, he seemed a hundred percent improved in his devotional life. That was because imagination put him in touch with prayer and meditation and stillness. As for his personal ministry in the world, his imagination afforded him a 60 percent increase in creative ways to live out his faith. And you know what? His imagination showed him that he had the solutions to many of his problems. The solutions were within him all the time: God had put them there. The sower started working on himself like a shade tree mechanic works on a car, and, lo and behold, he was at least 30 percent freer of problems than he had been before. Amen.